A NEW TEACHER'S GUIDE

Surviving Your First Year

Harvey Singer

A SCARECROWEDUCATION BOOK

The Scarecrow Press, Inc.
Lanham, Maryland, and Oxford
2003

A SCARECROWEDUCATION BOOK

Published in the United States of America
by Scarecrow Press, Inc.
A Member of the Rowman & Littlefield Publishing Group
4501 Forbes Boulevard, Suite 200, Lanham, Maryland 20706
www.scaroweducation.com

PO Box 317
Oxford
OX2 9RU, UK

British Library Cataloguing in Publication Information Available

Library of Congress Cataloging-in-Publication Data

Singer, Harvey, 1940–
  A new teacher's guide : surviving your first year / Harvey Singer.
    p. cm.
  "A ScarecrowEducation book."
  ISBN 0-8108-4573-3 (hardcover : alk. paper) — ISBN 0-8108-4574-1 (pbk :
alk. paper)
  1. First year teachers. 2. Teacher effectiveness. 1. Title: Surviving your first
year. II. Title.
  LB2844. 1.N4 S56 2003
  371.1—dc21

                                                                    2002011766

⊗™ The paper used in this publication meets the minimum requirements of
American National Standard for Information Sciences—Permanence of Paper
for Printed Library Materials, ANSI/NISO Z39.48-1992.
Manufactured in the United States of America.

CONTENTS

ACKNOWLEDGMENTS

This book could never have happened were it not for the many great teachers whom I have known, as a student, a teacher, and as an administrator. But it is also a tribute to the many, many good teachers, very good teachers actually, who teach their classes day in and day out, sometimes under less than ideal conditions, and sometimes for salaries that are not commensurate with their training, ability, and dedication. And it is also a tribute to the many school administrators who are sensitive to the needs of their staffs, their students, and their communities, and by whose support, their teachers are enabled and encouraged to be the best teachers that they can possibly be.

Teaching is both a craft and an art, and unfortunately I can never name everyone from whom I have learned my craft and my art—there are many too many of them. But I would like to mention some of the people who have been of invaluable assistance with the preparation of this book.

Stephen Schneider, Leo Polaski, Pat Lacerva, Stuart Singer, and Madine Singer each read the manuscript, and offered their very perceptive insights and their encouragement, and I am fortunate for their help, and especially to have them as treasured friends. Neal Postman, one of the truly great teachers I have had the privilege of knowing, also read the manuscript and encouraged me along the way. And David Kravetz, an attorney and professor of law, another dear friend and a remarkable teacher, also read and critiqued the manuscript, and was particularly helpful in regard to some of the legal issues.

I cannot neglect to mention my son Jonathan, a young teacher himself, with whom I have spent many hours "talking shop"—some of these chapters had their inspiration during some of those conversations. Nor can I neglect to mention my daughter Jacqueline, who also read the manuscript and offered her unique insights.

And finally, my parents Al and Helen Singer, who by their words and deeds taught me, from a very early age, about caring for and about other people, and in a very real sense made my career, and this book, possible.

FIRST THOUGHTS

Experience is what you get when you were expecting something else.

A friend of mine, a doctor, once told me that he learned more about medicine in his first year of practice than he learned in four years of medical school. I mentioned that to another friend, an attorney, and he said that he learned more about law in his first year of practice than he learned in three years of law school. Obviously, you cannot become a doctor without going to medical school or an attorney without going to law school. But there is an awful lot about being good at what you do, and successful, and even about survival, that you can only learn by "doing it."

Of course, the same is true of teaching. You have learned your subject matter in college. And you have learned a lot of methods and techniques in "Ed. Courses." But your first year of teaching is likely to be the most difficult, and challenging, and perhaps even the most exciting year of your entire career. And you will probably learn more about teaching in that first year than you have learned in your four years of college. In fact, you may find that you learn more about the practical aspects of day-to-day teaching in that first year than you will learn in any other single year of your next thirty-five to forty years as a teacher.

In this book, I will share with you some of the essence of what I have learned over the course of my many years as a successful teacher. It is based on my experiences as an English teacher, first in an inner city junior high school, and then in a large city high school. And it is also based on my work as a high school Dean of Students, a school counselor, a school administrator, a college instructor, and a college administrator.

Obviously, I have learned a lot along the way. And I would like to share what I have learned, the practical "stuff," to help you get through your first year. No, not just to get through your first year, but to be really successful. I hope that this book helps you to become the best teacher that you can, in the shortest possible time.

Of all the jobs I have held, teaching was the best—the most challenging and the most rewarding. That is not to say that there have not been challenges, and sometimes frustrations, along the way. But still, it is without a doubt the best job that I have ever had.

I hope that you will feel the same way about your career, and wish you much success as a teacher. I hope that you will find teaching as exciting as it has been for me—and that as you progress, and learn, and become really good at what you do, that you will never miss an opportunity to share the wisdom that you have acquired with the next generation of teachers.

A Brief Note: In most cases I have used the pronoun "he" to refer to teachers, students, administrators, and parents. It was just easier and less awkward than referring to, "he and she." Please do not take that as anything more or less than stylistic and grammatical expediency.

THE FIRST DAY

The only Zen you find on the tops of mountains is the Zen you bring up there.

It was my first day as a teacher. Oh, of course I had been a student teacher. But this was my first day as a "real teacher." The school was a junior high school in the South Bronx area of New York City, a school that at best could be referred to as "challenging."

I can't say that it was the best place that I ever worked. Admittedly, some days were rewarding—even fun. Most often though, teaching there was challenging, and often too, it was frustrating. But I learned a lot there—an awful lot. And many of the lessons that I learned were an important step in my development as a teacher.

It's funny how that old, worn building looked new and fresh to me that first day. I suppose it was, in large part, due to my excitement and enthusiasm. As I entered the building, the first person I encountered was a seasoned teacher, a middle-aged man carrying a stack of textbooks that towered over him.

He introduced himself, and I could not help but imagine that he had been a teacher there for a long, long time. And without hesitating, he told me that he was going to share with me the secret of being a successful teacher.

"Check your attendance first thing in the morning and send it to the office immediately," he cautioned me, "and they will never bother you." "Most likely," he continued," they'll never even observe you teach a class." Without hesitating, he continued, "But turn in your attendance cards even ten minutes late, and they'll never leave you alone."

I laughed to myself. Could that be all it took to be a successful teacher at this school? Was this man right, or was he just a cynic?

The answer is, I am sure, both. "They," the school administration, certainly did seem to "bother" teachers who turned in their daily attendance reports late. And they also seemed to not much bother those who turned them in promptly.

I did heed his advice, and the administration never bothered me. Oh, they did observe me teach a class from time to time. But they did so very infrequently.

Of course, there is a lot more to being a successful teacher than just turning in your attendance reports, and your other paperwork, on time. But there's definitely some wisdom here.

The collective wisdom in a school is an amazing source of information. Listen to your experienced colleagues. But never assume that one teacher, or even the collective wisdom, is necessarily right. Or that even if it is right, that it is necessarily right for you.

❸

THE TECHNICAL SIDE OF LEARNING

Better than a thousand days of diligent study, is one day with a great teacher.

Japanese Proverb

HOW LEARNING HAPPENS

I had graduated from college and had taught for a year, and I was taking graduate courses at New York University. One of my professors, a man whom I had gotten to know socially told me one day, "You must take a course with Jack Robertson." So I did.

It was one of those accelerated summer courses, four hours a day, five days a week, for two weeks. You took a midterm at the end of the first week, and at the end of the second week you turned in a term paper and sat for the final exam. Most of the students were teachers like me. I'm certain that the schedule was as demanding for the professor as it was for the students

Professor Robertson began each class with a lecture about an issue in teaching, and then opened the floor to discussion. After about two hours, with the discussion in full swing, Professor Robertson would say, "Let's take a thirty-minute break."

There was a sit-down coffee shop just across the street, and while it wasn't required, everyone in the class went there. Students sat at tables in small groups, and the discussions, while casual, were virtually always continuations of the discussion that had begun in class that day. Jack Robertson sat with a different group of students each day.

At some point, Professor Robertson would stand up and leave. That unspoken signal indicated that the break had ended, and everyone returned to class. Back in the classroom, Professor Robertson asked, "What did you talk about during the break?" And the discussion continued, this time in the classroom.

Those discussions were not only interesting, they were incredibly insightful. I learned a lot about teaching from Professor Robertson, and from my classmates, both philosophically and practically. And while I learned much of it in class, I also learned a great deal during those discussions at the coffee shop.

And I also learned, from the way that Jack Robertson conducted his class, that much of the learning that takes place in any class takes place outside the classroom. And that that learning isn't only what occurs when students are studying for examinations or preparing term papers. Encourage your students to continue their exploration of the class material outside of class, and then to share what they have learned with their classmates. They will learn much, much more than you can ever teach them in your classroom.

THE ANSWER

Another professor who had a significant impact on my teaching was Howard Damon, also at the New York University Graduate School of Education. I don't remember the exact title of the course, but it was a "methods" class. Like Professor Robertson's class, this was also a summer class, but it met for fewer hours each day and continued for longer. But as in Professor Robertson's class, practically everyone in the class had spent at least one year teaching English.

Professor Damon began the first class by asking how one taught students to learn the meaning of unfamiliar words that they encountered while they were reading.

Someone said that he taught his students to become proficient at using the dictionary. Someone else suggested that she spent time teaching word roots, prefixes, and suffixes. And still someone else suggested that she taught students to discover the meanings of words from the context in which they appeared. Professor Damon wrote each suggestion on the board. Then he proceeded to discuss each one in turn.

First, he asked how many of us routinely looked up the meanings of words that we did not know in the dictionary. Only one or two hands went up. He commented, "If you're English teachers, and you don't routinely look up words that you don't know in the dictionary, how can you expect your students to do it?"

Then he wrote a word on the chalkboard. The root and prefix were familiar to most of the English teachers in the room. But the meaning of the word was elusive. "Obviously, he commented, "that doesn't work."

Of course, when he wrote the word in a sentence, even in context, its meaning remained elusive.

At about that point, Professor Damon indicated that the class time was over. Before we left, someone asked, "But how do you teach students to find the meanings or words that they don't know. What is the answer?"

Professor Damon replied, "You're the English teachers. I'm sure that you can figure it out."

I'm sure that there are at least two important lessons here:

1. The obvious answers to questions are not always correct. Often, in fact, the answers that we take for granted, the answers that we always "knew" were correct, may not be correct.
2. It is often better to let students discover answers for themselves, than to "feed" the right answers to them. Of course, this is not always possible. But when it is, students are much more likely to remember answers that they have discovered for themselves. And, as a further advantage, the process of asking questions and discovering answers will enable them to think more critically and creatively, not just in your class, but for the rest of their lives.

On a very practical level, think about some of the things about teaching and about your subject matter that you are absolutely certain are right. Are you absolutely certain that they are? And also, think about ways to encourage your students to discover the answers to questions for themselves, rather than by telling them the answers.

THE DEVELOPMENTAL LESSON

It would be foolish to think that there is one best way to teach anything. To be sure, there are many good ways to teach any lesson, and, of course, there are also some ways that are not quite as good. The best approach is one that is consistent with your personal teaching style and the specific material you are teaching, and is appropriate for the particular students you are teaching.

That said, there is one type of lesson that almost always works in the secondary grades, and is also often appropriate in the lower grades. It looks particularly good to onlookers when, for example, you are being observed. This lesson is often referred to as the developmental lesson, and you will probably find it a welcome addition to your personal bag of tricks.

The developmental lesson has several distinct parts:

1. An Introduction—often a question, but sometimes an interesting story.
2. The Aim—quite simply the lesson's objective, an outgrowth of the question or story that was presented in the Introduction.
3. Questions—which lead to a better understanding of the Aim, and perhaps, an answer to the question that was asked in the Introduction.
4. A Medial Summary—a review somewhere near the lesson's midpoint.
5. Additional Questions—which continue the search for an understanding of the Aim.
6. A Final Summary—which refers back to the Question and Aim, and actually answers the Question.

Let's take a look at the individual parts of the developmental lesson.

Introduction

Begin the lesson with an introduction, often an interesting question or story. The purpose of the introduction is to present your students with a question or problem, and also to motivate them to want to find the answer to the question.

For example, suppose that you were teaching Robert Frost's poem, "Mending Wall" to an English class. You might begin by asking students whether it is a good idea to have a fence around one's home. Try to get a variety of responses on both sides of the issue, but don't look for an in-depth discussion. Remember, your purpose here is to introduce the topic to your students, and to pique their interest. The entire process should be brief—don't spend more than about five minutes on the Introduction.

The Aim

The aim is the objective of the lesson, and should be an outgrowth of the Introduction. It may be a formal statement of the question, or a statement of what the students will attempt to discover in the course of the lesson. When you formalize the aim with your students, write it on the board, and do not erase it until the lesson has been completed.

In this case, the aim might be, "Is it a good idea to have fences around out homes?" Of course, you might say that the aim is to read and understand Robert Frost's poem. And you are certainly correct about that. But that isn't a very interesting aim. And besides, don't you also want your students to understand themselves and life a little better as a result of having read and understood the poem?

Questioning—I

After stating the aim, you will present the material in the lesson, largely by asking your students a series of questions that will lead them, in small steps, to the answer to the question. In this case, students will read and analyze the poem.

If you don't remember this poem, it begins, "Something there is that doesn't love a wall." What is the "something" that doesn't like walls? And then, why do you think the poet used the word "love," rather than, "like"? Why did the poet not say, "People just don't like walls"?

Small steps, students learn best in small steps. And to be sure that they remember the important steps that they have taken, note them on the board.

Medial Summary

OK, "medial" is a pedantic word. But it sounds better than the "halfway point" summary. Approximately halfway through the lesson you will usually present a medial summary. That is, you or a student, or a few students, will restate what has been learned to that point, and you will also remind students of the aim of the lesson. While you will find that it is generally desirable to have a medial summary, in some lessons you may choose to omit this step.

Questioning—2

After the medial summary, you will continue asking questions, which will ultimately result in your class arriving at an answer to the question that you asked in the Aim, or if the Aim is not a question, to a better understanding of it.

Final Summary

The final summary will review the material that your class has covered, will refer back to the Aim. "Is it a good idea to have fences around our homes?" I am certain that your students will find a lot of interesting questions to explore:

"Why are fences a good idea?"

"Why are they not?"

"What other kinds of fences are there?"

"Do we sometimes build 'fences' around ourselves?"

I'll bet, that if you did a good job, some of the discussions will continue after class. I'll bet that your students will come away from this lesson understanding not only Robert Frost's poem, but life, a little better than before it began.

Remember that there is no one best type of lesson. But the developmental lesson almost always works, and it almost always looks really good to observers. Make it your showcase lesson, and you are almost guaranteed to receive rave reviews from observers.

THE ART OF QUESTIONING—AND TIMING

The secret of teaching, if there is one secret, is that students learn much, much better by figuring things out for themselves than they do by being told. Of course, there is no way that a student can figure out that the battle of Hastings, for example, took place in 1066. But they can figure out some of the implications of that event. And if they do, what they have figured out—learned—will make it more likely that they will be able to apply what they have learned to other questions, and to other facets of their lives. And isn't that, after all, is what effective teaching is all about?

That is why questioning is such an important part of teaching. The successful teacher decides what he wants his students to learn, and then constructs a series of questions that will lead them to the answer. And the best questioning leads students to the final answer in very small steps.

Questioning has another advantage. Ask questions that your students can answer, and praise their answers, and they will not only learn what you want them to learn, but you will also improve their self-esteem. And because they are achieving success, your students will want to answer more of your questions. That's right, learn the art of successful questioning, and your students will not only work harder, they will actually want to work harder!

But there is another aspect of questioning that makes some teachers much better at it than others. Have you ever noticed that some people can never tell a joke successfully? It isn't that their material isn't funny. It's that their presentation is faulty. And the most common reason that some people can't tell jokes effectively is that their timing is off. To tell a joke successfully, the punch line not only has to be funny, it has to come at just the right moment—often after a moment's hesitation.

The next time you see a comedian, pay attention not only to what he is saying, but also to his timing. You are sure to notice that timing, as much as the actual jokes themselves, is what makes some comedians much funnier than others.

Timing is also an important part of questioning. When you ask your class a question, don't call on a student for an immediate answer. Wait a moment so that everyone has a chance to think about it. Then call on someone for the answer. Work on both your questioning and your timing if you want to become a truly effective teacher.

Does that sound like I am saying that as a teacher, you are a performer? It certainly does. And you certainly are!

LEARNING THEIR NAMES

Some teachers learn students' names easily, but others do so with great difficulty. And, obviously, most secondary school teachers have to learn many more students' names than most primary grade teachers do. But regardless of how many students you teach, and regardless of whether you find it easy or hard to learn your students' names, make a sincere effort to do so as quickly as possible. Not only will this help with your classroom management and control, but it will also show your students that you think that they are important—important enough for you to take the time to learn their names.

One effective technique is to draw a grid or seating chart that represents your classroom on a sheet of paper. Each student desk or work area is represented by a box on the grid. Write each student's name in the appropriate box and refer to the seating chart as you call on students. After a few class sessions, you should remember most if not all of your students' names.

An added advantage of creating a seating chart is that in the event that you are absent from school it will be invaluable to the substitute teacher who covers your class.

When I began teaching in New York City many years ago, Delaney Books were a very popular item. In fact, most New York City schools distributed Delaney Books to teachers, and virtually all the teachers that I knew used them.

A Delaney book is a book in which the pages contain slots representing each student desk or workstation. In the primary grades, a teacher needs only one page, but in the secondary grades, the book contains a separate page for each of the teacher's classes.

At the beginning of the year, each student enters their name and some identifying information on a Delaney card, a small card that measures about 1¼" by 3". Most commonly, students write their name, address, and telephone number in appropriate sections on the front of the card, and their name on the back. The teacher then inserts the cards into the slots, which represent each student's desk or work area.

The Delaney Book made it easy to learn students' names. And if you changed a student's seat, it was easy to simply move the student's Delaney Card to the new appropriate slot.

The back of the Delaney card was reddish in color, and contained a row for each month and the numbers of the days in each month. At the beginning of the class, the teacher checked the attendance. If a student was absent, the teacher turned over the student's Delaney Card and drew a line through the date, providing a record of the student's attendance in class. If the student arrived late, the teacher simply drew a circle around the line that he had drawn through the date.

Delaney Books and Delaney Cards have never been particularly popular in schools outside of New York City. However, many teachers find them a wonderful, low-tech way to help them learn students' names, and also to keep track of the students in their classes and their attendance. If the idea appeals to you, ask your school supply representative about ordering one. Or see if your school will order one for you.

TEACHING A DIFFICULT CLASS

Often, teachers are assigned difficult classes early in their teaching careers. It isn't that your school administrator wants to challenge you—it's more a matter that practically no one wants to teach difficult classes. And while more seasoned teachers could probably teach difficult classes more effectively than novice teachers, most experienced teachers prefer, and find it more rewarding, to teach what are seen as "easier" classes.

There are a number of things that you can do to be successful with difficult classes. Actually, some of my most rewarding experiences have been with classes and students that many teachers would consider difficult. In fact, one of the best teachers and administrators that I have ever known, Peter Micera, almost always chose to teach classes with students which most teachers would consider "difficult." You may find that you feel the same way.

The first secret of working effectively with a difficult class is organization and routines. Tell students exactly what you expect of them, and "get down to business" very quickly. For example, in a high school math class students may begin every class session by doing a few practice examples that you have written on the board. Since they only have five minutes to complete the practice examples, your students must get to their seats and do them immediately. If you collect and grade them on a random basis, students will always begin working quickly.

Immediately after the exercises, discuss the answers and then move on to homework assignments—and from there, to the new work. The idea is to have established routines, and to keep students too busy to be difficult.

The second secret of working with a difficult class is to give the students many, many opportunities to be successful, and to praise them whenever they are successful. Make them feel good about themselves and their progress, and they will not only work hard, they will love you.

A Few Words about Praise

You have to be honest when you praise students, and your praise has to be related to your goals for them. Don't say, "Good answer," or "Good homework" if a student's answer or his homework isn't good—he, as well as all your other students, will learn not to trust you. And while praising a student's new shirt, for example, may help to establish a relationship with him, which is certainly desirable, praising a student's good work will certainly be more productive in getting him to work harder.

When you have learned these tricks you may find that "difficult" classes are not nearly as difficult as most teachers think. And because they're less likely to be sophisticated or jaded, you may find that you actually prefer difficult classes to their "easier" counterparts.

STARTING TOUGH

It's the first day of school. One teacher is very businesslike. He spends a considerable amount of time explaining the curriculum that his class will be studying, and also his expectations, classroom rules, and procedures. There is an air of seriousness in the air, and most of the students leave the class with expectations that this class is not going to be fun.

Meanwhile, just across the hall another teacher is explaining the curriculum, and also his expectations, rules and procedures to his class. But he also tells them that the atmosphere is going to be casual, and that they are going to have fun learning the course material. Most of the students are smiling as they leave the room.

When I first started teaching, a veteran teacher told me to be very tough with my classes at the beginning of the year. "It's much easier," he said, "to ease up later than to try to gain control of a class than has become unruly." I still hear this from many teachers today. And I know many teachers who run their classes that way. I'm sure that there is more than a kernel of truth here.

However, I'm not sure that being tough early on will keep a class that is bent on being unruly from becoming unruly. And while it is probably true that it is harder to "tame" a class that has gotten out of control than to keep them from getting out of control in the first place, I'm not sure that being tough is the only way to prevent classroom problems. I think it is entirely possible to be friendly and still expect and insist that your students act appropriately.

Still, if being tough early in the year makes sense to you, there is certainly no reason not to do it. I would just suggest that while you are being firm, you be careful that you are not also being unreasonable. And always remember, however you choose to run your class, to treat your students with courtesy and respect. It is certainly possible to be firm and reasonable and respectful, all at the same time.

In the final analysis, teach in the way that is most comfortable for you. And understand that while it is possible to become less firm as the year progresses, it is also possible, although perhaps a little harder, to become more firm.

Once again, there is no one best way to teach. The best way is to teach in the way that works best for you.

PREPARING EXAMS

I recently saw the following bumper sticker:

> ### As Long As There Are Tests
> ### There Will Be Prayer in Schools

Tests are obviously an intrinsic part of the educational process.

Many years ago, I was a student teacher at The Bronx High School of Science in New York. The English Department Chairperson, Mr. Max Nadel, was one of the best supervisors I have ever worked for. Every time he watched me teach a lesson he complimented me on the lesson. And then, he offered some real insights into how I could have taught the lesson even more effectively.

One day a teacher became sick during the school day. Max asked me if I would cover one of her classes. He said that he would come into the class at some point to see how things were going.

I taught the class, but Max never arrived. When I returned to the English Department Office after the class had ended, I asked him why he had not visited the class. He said, "I looked in through the classroom window as I walked by, and I could tell that good things were going on inside."

Just as Max Nadel knew what kinds of things were going on in a classroom without ever setting his foot inside the door, every good administrator knows which teachers are teaching effectively, and which teachers need some assistance. And as your administrator most likely knows what kind of job you are doing in your classroom, you know how your individual students are performing without ever testing them.

But still, Max Nadel did often observe me teach, as he observed all the teachers on his staff. Most schools require administrators to formally observe their teachers at least several times each year. And as a teacher, even though you know a great deal about your students' performance by just watching them, you will frequently need to test them to formally evaluate their performance and progress. Teaching requires that you obtain some objective measurements of your students' progress.

New teachers often spend a considerable amount of time preparing examinations. And while they work hard at developing good tests, they are sometimes less than completely effective.

Here are some suggestions about testing, based on my experience as a teacher:

1. Your first step in creating a test is to determine exactly what you want to measure. That is not always as obvious as it may seem. In an English class, do you want to determine whether your students have learned the vocabulary words that you have assigned, or do you want to learn if they can use them appropriately? In a history class, do you want to know if your students know that the Battle of Hastings took place in 1066, or do you want them to know the implications of that event? Of course, there is no right answer here. Sometimes you will want to know if your students know the facts that you have taught them, and sometimes you will want to know if they can use those facts.

2. What kind of test questions will best determine if your students have learned what you have taught them? Short answer questions are ideal for determining whether students have learned the facts. But there are a number of different kinds of short answer questions: fill-ins, multiple-choice, true-false, match-up. Each serves a slightly different purpose—fill-ins, for example, require a different degree of mastery than multiple-choice questions.

3. Essay questions measure how well your students can use facts and make inferences. And they also measure how well students can organize information, and how well they can write. Grading them, unfortunately, is much more subjective. And grading essay questions is much more time-consuming than grading short answer questions.

4. Always include a few easy questions. You want even your weakest students to be able to achieve some measure of success on your exams. Remember that students who have no chance of being successful often give up completely. Or even worse, they seek attention in other, less acceptable ways.

5. Of course, you will also want to provide some difficult questions. If a number of students each achieve a perfect score, your test will not enable you to distinguish between them.

6. Evaluate correct and incorrect answers. If many students get the same question wrong, there are only two possible explanations:
   a. it was a poor question, or
   b. you need to re-teach that material.

If the former is true, you want to disregard the question. And if it is the latter, you will certainly want to reteach the topic.

7. Prepare your examinations with an eye to grading them. You spend a considerable amount of time preparing for your classes and teaching them. When you prepare an examination, always give some thought to designing it in a way that will make it easier to grade. For example, in a section of multiple choice questions you might want to arrange the choices so that the correct answers form an easily remembered pattern, say: a, b, c, a, b, c, a, a, b, b. Think of how much easier it will be for you to grade that section of the test.

STRESS AND PERFORMANCE

You've probably heard it said a thousand times, "People work better un-under stress." Is it true, or is it a myth?

Many years ago, when a caveman was threatened he experienced both physical and psychological changes that enabled him to better deal with the situation. His heart rate and blood pressure rose, the pupils of his eyes dilated, blood flow was diverted from his digestive system to his arms and legs, and the ability of his blood to clot improved. In addition to these physical changes, he became more alert and mentally energized. The combination of these physical and emotional changes enabled the caveman to better confront the threat, or to escape from it. Consequently, this is called the "fight or flight" response.

So it would seem that stress enables people to perform both physical and mental tasks better. And if that is the case, there are certainly implications for education. There are, however, two significant problems in regard to stress:

1. In our society, many people are stressed all the time, or almost all the time.
2. The physical and emotional changes that take place when people are under stress can have very serious physical and emotional consequences.

Many people are stressed all the time.

When we think of people who are stressed all the time, we generally think of people in business, constantly striving to meet deadlines and goals. But for most people who are in a constant state of stress, the problem began much earlier in their lives.

Think about the ambitious high school student who is determined to get accepted to a very selective college. He works very hard to maintain an outstanding academic record, is involved in a number of school and community activities, may play an instrument in the school band, may be a member of one or more teams, and may have a part-time job. And this doesn't even begin to take into account his family responsibilities. Of course, he's under a great deal of stress. And the stress almost never ends.

The physical and emotional changes that take place when people are under stress can have very serious physical and emotional consequences.

After the caveman dealt with a stressful situation, either by confronting it or escaping from it, the stress ended and his body was able to return to its normal state. But when people are under almost constant stress, as many people are today, their bodies never have a chance to recover and they begin to suffer from a considerable number of physical and emotional problems. Doctors continue to discover that many medical problems are caused by stress. But even for conditions for which stress is not the major cause, it is, at the very least, a contributing factor.

The implications for your students should be obvious. Stress may enable them to perform better at some tasks—how much better is controversial. But in many cases, the increased performance will be more than offset by the physical and emotional toll that it exacts. And perhaps even more significant, if our young people are exposed to almost constant stress now, do they have any chance of escaping from the pattern as they become adults?

As a teacher, you have no control over the stress that is imposed on your students from outside your classroom. And, you also have no control over the self-imposed stress that some students bring to your classroom. But you do exert a considerable degree of control over the amount of stress that you impose on them. And it seems to me, when you consider the big picture, that stress is more likely to be counter-productive than otherwise.

4

THE PERSONAL SIDE OF LEARNING

The secret of education is respecting the pupil.

Ralph Waldo Emerson

THE PERSONAL SIDE OF LEARNING

The following has been circulated around the Internet for some time. If you haven't seen it, it involves taking a short quiz.

1. Name the five wealthiest people in the world.
2. Name the last five Heisman trophy winners.
3. Name the last five winners of the Miss America contest.
4. Name ten people who have won the Nobel or Pulitzer prize.
5. Name the last half dozen Academy Award winners for best actor/actress.
6. Name the last decade's worth of World Series winners.

How did you do?

Probably not very well. The point is that few of us remember yesterday's headlines for very long. And we are talking here about people who are among the very best in their fields. But then the applause dies, the achievements forgotten, and daily life goes on.

Here's another quiz. See how you do on this one:

1. List a few teachers who were really important to you.
2. Name three friends who have helped you through really difficult times.
3. Name five people who have taught you something worthwhile.
4. Think of a few people who have made you feel appreciated and special.
5. Think of five people you enjoy spending time with.

Of course, the second set of questions are easier.

And, of course, there is a lesson here. The people who make a difference in our lives are not the ones with the most credentials, the most money, or the most awards. *They are the ones that care.*

As the late President John F. Kennedy said,

> Few will have the greatness to bend history itself, but each of us can work to change a small portion of events, and in the total of all those acts will be written the history of this generation.

There is no Nobel Prize or Congressional Medal of Honor for teaching. Yet many teachers, many, many teachers, are more important in the lives of their students than many of the people who are far better known, and who receive many more accolades. Never underestimate the tremendous impact that you have on your students—and will have, for the rest of their lives.

STUDENTS WHO THINK THEY WILL SUCCEED INVARIABLY DO

Albert Einstein once said, "It should be possible to teach the laws of physics to a barmaid." That is, of course, assuming that you have a barmaid who wants to learn the laws of physics.

Assume that you have found a suitable barmaid. And assume, also, that she is not a physics major, tending bar part-time while she completes her doctoral dissertation on quantum mechanics. Your first step will be to determine specifically what concepts you want to teach her, and then, to establish a suitable order in which to present them—in other words, you will create a curriculum. And then, of course, you will also need to spend some time developing suitable ways to present the material that you want her to learn—techniques that are appropriate not only for your subject matter, but also for your audience.

But the best curriculum and the best presentation are not nearly enough. The single most important factor in education is to convince the student that he, or in this case she, will master the material. Notice that I said "will" master the material. Not "can." Can is just not good enough. The same is true in your classroom, where you can convince students that they can master the material you are teaching in two distinct ways.

The first is by telling your students that they will be successful. On the first day of class, I tell my students that I have never had a student who has:

1. attended class regularly,
2. done their assignments, and
3. failed the class.

"That is," I assure them, "this course comes with a guarantee—if you attend and do the work, you will pass."

But telling your students that they will be successful is only the first part of the equation. You must also show them, very frequently, that they are succeeding. Ask them questions that they can answer, and praise them for their correct answers. In fact, praise them even for incorrect answers. "That's not what I was looking for, but your answer certainly shows that you're on the right track." And be sure to include at least some questions in every lesson, and on every exam, that even your weakest students can answer correctly.

What happens if a student attends class regularly and does all the required assignments, but still fails to master the work? I maintain that this will rarely if ever happen. I assure you that in many, many years of teaching it has never happened in any of my classes—not even once.

But what if it does? Certainly, I can't tell you how to grade a student in this situation. But I do know that one possible way of handling this situation on the secondary or college level is to assign the lowest passing grade to the student, and to counsel the student, very sensitively, that it would probably be in his best interests not to take additional courses in this discipline.

In the lower grades, perhaps such a student has a learning disability that needs to be investigated by the school counselor or psychologist. But in those cases, you've probably already done that.

SHOW THEM THAT YOU LIKE THEM

I wish I knew who it was that wrote, "They may forget what you said, but they will never forget how you made them feel." I am absolutely certain that this is true, not only in teaching, but in all of life. But I am certain that it is particularly true in the relationship between students and teachers. Think about it. Who were the most memorable teachers in your life? I'll bet that they were not necessarily the best teachers (although most of them probably were). I'll bet that they were the teachers who made you feel the best about yourself.

I am not suggesting that teaching is a popularity contest, and I am not suggesting that you become your students' friend. Certainly, I would hope that your students will like you, and that they will respect you. But your success as a teacher will depend, to a large degree, on the extent to which you can make your students feel good about themselves. And probably the most important thing that you can do toward accomplishing that is showing your students that you like them.

The reason should be obvious. It has long been accepted that students who believe that they can succeed at learning invariably do. Tell a student . . . no convince him . . . that he will learn what you are about to teach him, and his chances of success are near one hundred percent.

The converse is also true. I once took a continuing education course in which the instructor began the first session by saying that in her experience two thirds of the students who registered for the class would not complete it. She was absolutely correct in her prediction.

But I am equally certain that she was correct every time that she taught the class.

Certainly, her material and teaching techniques could have been much better than they were. But her true failure as a teacher, and it was she who was the failure, not her students, was in large part due to her opening remarks. She told her students that most of them would not succeed, they believed it, and they lived up to her expectations.

Certainly, you are teaching subject matter to your students. But they are also learning, or they should be learning, how to think critically, how to interact with each other and other people, and how to work cooperatively—both with other students and with adults.

Long after they have forgotten the history, or mathematics, or science that you have taught them, they will "remember" how they interacted with their classmates, and with you, and they will carry that learning with them for the rest of their lives.

Never lose sight of the fact that, "They may forget what you said, but they will never forget how you made them feel," and you are certain to be an incredibly successful teacher. And, as an added bonus, your students will be much more likely to remember the subject matter that you have taught them.

DON'T EVER EMBARRASS A STUDENT

As Dean of Students at a New York City high school, I occasionally had to discipline a student who had been disrespectful to a teacher. The most serious of these cases occurred in a classroom where the student was defiant to the teacher in plain sight of other students.

Of course, I always relied on the teacher to provide me with a description of what had happened. But in my discussion with the student, I always began by asking him to tell me, from his perspective, what had happened. Then, we talked about why he could never again speak to that teacher, or any teacher, in that way. I wanted the student to understand why that kind of behavior was totally unacceptable, and I also wanted him to know, unequivocally, that it would not be tolerated.

In most cases the student agreed to apologize to the teacher. He usually did that just before class began, privately, but in view of the other students. I didn't want the student to be embarrassed in front of his classmates, but it was also important for the other students in the class to know that he was apologizing for what he had done.

If the incident was particularly serious, I would punish the student in some way that was apparent to other students: a parent conference, after-school detention, in-school suspension, or occasionally, even, suspension from school. The student, of course, needed to know that this type of behavior was unacceptable. And just as important, the other students in the class needed to know that there were consequences for the student's actions so that they would be less likely to act in a similar way.

Generally, students understood that being disrespectful to a teacher was a serious offence, and recurrences were relatively rare. But some situations were particularly difficult to resolve.

This was particularly true when the teacher had said or done something that embarrassed the student in front of the class. I remember one teacher who routinely embarrassed students in her classes. Certainly, when there were problems, her students' defiant responses were inappropriate. But what they had done was completely understandable, even predictable, because to some degree, a very significant degree, the teacher was responsible for the problem. When you put a student in a situation in which he feels that he is losing face in front of his peers, you are asking for trouble.

It is difficult, if not impossible, to convince a student that he cannot be disrespectful to a teacher when the teacher has been disrespectful to him, and particularly when the teacher has been openly disrespectful to the student. Most teachers, of course, are very sensitive to this. But some aren't. And those teachers create problems for themselves, their students, and often other teachers as well.

Think about it. Try really hard never to embarrass a student. And if you inadvertently do, apologize . . . quickly and sincerely.

John has come to class, once again, without his notebook or a pen. In frustration, you say, "John, what's wrong with you?" Or perhaps, inadvertently, you say something even worse.

You realize immediately that you should not have said that. So before John has a chance to react, you say something like, "I'm really sorry I said that, John. I was frustrated that you came to class unprepared again. But that's no excuse for what I said. I'm sorry that I said it, and it won't happen again."

You won't lose John's respect—most likely, you will gain it. And just as importantly, you will gain the respect of all your students. As an added bonus, you will have taught them an incredibly valuable lesson about life. And, it is even more likely that John will remember to bring his notebook and pen to class in the future.

GROWING UP IN DIFFERENT TIMES

"Do not confine your children to your own learning, for they were born in another time." Hebrew Proverb.

Life is certainly very different from what it was 100 years ago, or 50 years ago, or even 20 years ago. And in more ways than one, that can have a major impact on your day-to-day teaching.

When I tell my students, for example, that the Internet developed in the way that it did because it was created in 1969, during the "cold war," that statement means very little, if anything, to them. Even if my students are familiar with the term "cold war," they don't really know what it means. They don't know that in those days students in many schools participated in air-raid drills during which they had to hide under their desks or in hallways away from windows. They will only know it, if I, or someone else, tells them.

Keep in mind that your students' experiences, and their knowledge about life and culture, are in some respects very, very different from yours. In fact, they may even be different, in some very significant ways, from those of their younger or older brothers and sisters. And when you refer to these kinds of issues, take the time to explain them, not just in factual terms, but also in terms of feelings, emotions, beliefs, and values. And remember, too, that your students, because of their cultural differences, may even see some current issues very differently from the way you see them.

Whenever you recognize that these issues and differences exist, try to explore them in real terms. Encourage your students to discuss them with older family members, and don't hesitate to share your own relevant experiences with your students.

DEVELOP CLASS SPIRIT

Whether you like it or not, we live in a highly competitive society. Many people work at competitive jobs and are also competitive in any of a variety of leisure activities. And then, of course, the widespread interest in professional sports adds to the competitive nature of our society. So it should come as no surprise that in many ways most schools are reasonably competitive places.

I am not suggesting that competitiveness in school is necessarily good or bad. One can easily argue either side of that issue. But the fact is that competition is already an undeniable fact of life. And since it is already there, I am not at all adverse to using it to help improve the learning that goes on in my classroom.

A fairly easy way to do this is to encourage your class to be the very best class in the school. Note that I did not suggest that you encourage your students to be the smartest students in the school, or even the best readers or math students in the school, but rather, to be the best class in the school. That is, the best behaved, most creative, friendliest, and most hard-working class.

Convince your students that they want to be the best class in the school (this is probably more achievable in the younger grades, and perhaps middle school, than in high school classes), and they will rise to the occasion. Convince them that they are already the best, and they will work especially hard to prove that you are right, and to continue to be the best.

And, of course, if your students are the best students in the school, you cannot help but look good yourself.

"I REMEMBER YOUR OLDER BROTHER"

If you had an older brother or sister, at least one of your teachers has undoubtedly said to you, "I remember your older brother (or sister). He (or she) was. . . .

In fact, it probably happened more times than you care to remember. How did you feel about it? You probably hated hearing it, because it's a "no win" situation. If your older sibling was a good student, you wondered if you could ever live up to his reputation. And if he wasn't, you wondered if you were doomed to mediocrity in your teacher's mind from the outset.

It doesn't take long to have taught in a school long enough to have taught the older brothers and sisters of some of your current students. It can happen in as little as only one or two years. Resist the urge to refer to your students' older siblings. Your students are sure to really appreciate the fact that you see them as completely unique individuals rather than as someone to be compared with someone else.

Certainly, there will be times when a student will refer to an older brother or sister who was a student of yours. Even when a student brings up the subject, be sensitive to it. Simply smile, and say, "Yes I remember him (or her). How is he (or she) doing? Please send my regards."

YOUR PERSONAL STYLE

When you have a chance, it's really nice to watch someone else teach a lesson, especially a really good lesson. But when you watch a colleague teach a lesson, there is a potential pitfall that you want to be aware of. You see the teacher teach a wonderful lesson, so the first chance you get, you teach the same lesson in the same way. Perhaps it is a success. But it is just as likely to be a flop.

There may be one best way to swing a golf club or a baseball bat— I don't know for certain, but I tend to doubt it. But I do know, with certainty, that there is no one best way to teach a lesson, any lesson. Certainly, there are better ways and there are ways that are not so good. But the best way to teach a lesson is the way that works for you, and that is an outgrowth of your personal style.

So never miss an opportunity to observe other teachers, and to learn from what you see them do. And that involves the teachers that you work with, as well as your memories of all the teachers who have been your teachers, from the earliest grades up through graduate school. Take the best of what you have seen and add it to your repertoire. But use it in a way that is consistent with your personality and your personal style, and always remember that what works for someone else may not work for you.

YOU CAN NEVER MAKE EVERYONE HAPPY

Dr. Neil Postman was one of my professors when I was a graduate student at New York University. In addition to having written a considerable number of very popular books, Dr. Postman was a great teacher. Not only were his classes incredibly interesting, but he also truly liked and respected his students.

I was really fortunate in getting to know Neil Postman personally. After I graduated, we used to arrange to meet periodically. Most often I would sit in on one of his late afternoon classes, and after the class we would have dinner at a local restaurant.

I remember once sitting in on one of his large, undergraduate classes. Most of the students in the class seemed to be as interested in Dr. Postman's lecture as I had always been, but a few students who were sitting in the back of the room were involved in other activities. One was doing a crossword puzzle, while another appeared to be doing an assignment for another class.

I wanted to scream at them, "You don't know what you are missing!" But, of course, I didn't scream at them. And even if I had, it is unlikely that it would have made any difference.

When I was a high school English teacher, at the end of every year I asked my students to write short, anonymous evaluations of the class. The evaluations were almost always very positive, and in addition to the positive feedback, every so often a student would make a comment that enabled me to become an even better teacher.

Of course, there were occasionally negative comments. One student once said, "You seem like a nice guy, but I don't think you are." He went on to say, "And, when you sit down, I can sometimes see the tops of your socks. Haven't you ever heard about over-the-calf socks?"

I was teaching them English the best way I knew how, and he was concerned about my socks!

The bottom line, no matter how good a teacher you are, is that you can never expect to make everyone happy. When you put your heart into your teaching and you encounter a student who doesn't like you, or even who doesn't think you are a good teacher, don't obsess about it. Even if a few students in some of your classes don't like you or your teaching style, let it go. Their feelings don't for a minute detract from the fact that you're a good teacher—perhaps even a great teacher.

GREAT TEACHERS

Thinking back, I have known a great many teachers in my life. You have also—we all have.

First there were all the teachers in whose classes I have been a student, starting with my kindergarten teacher, and continuing through the teacher of the last class I've taken. And then there are all the speakers I've listened to at seminars and conferences, and all the people who have ever shown me how to do something—they have all, in a very real sense, been my teachers.

And then, of course, there were, and are, all the teachers that I have worked with, and continue to work with, at a variety of schools. The list seems endless.

As I think back about the capabilities of all those teachers, I am struck by the fact that there is no standard distribution here, no bell-shaped curve with a preponderance of average teachers, and a relatively small but equal number of good and bad teachers.

Certainly I have known some poor teachers, a few even, who were incompetent. But they were few and far between. The vast majority of the teachers that I have known have been very, very competent. And more than a few have been outstanding—teachers whom I would consider great teachers.

There was my high school physics teacher, Max Sherrin. Mr. Sherrin loved physics, he loved teaching, and perhaps most of all he loved his students. And he had the uncanny ability of being able to make almost anything understandable. And Julius Hlavaty, one of my high school math teachers and chairperson of the Mathematics Department, was an equally impressive teacher and human being. Max Sherrin could certainly have taught the laws of physics to a barmaid, and Julius Hlavaty could have taught her calculus. And she would have loved it, and them, as virtually all of their students did.

And then there was "Colonel" Isaacs, my high school American history teacher. Despite his insistence, The Colonel was not a real southern colonel. I'm sure he wasn't even a southerner—or a colonel. But The Colonel was adamant that the Civil War was not a civil war. "A civil war involves a group of people trying to take over the government," he explained. "We never wanted to take over the government—all we wanted to do was to leave the Union." He insisted that we not refer to it as the Civil War, but rather, as "the Late, Lamented Struggle For Southern Independence." Certainly, Colonel Isaacs wasn't promoting the Confederacy. He was making us question, and think.

Of course, I cannot leave out my college philosophy instructor, Dr. Irani. Although his listing in the college catalog contained only his undergraduate degree from the University of Bombay, Dr. Irani had a variety of degrees and experiences in a wide variety of disciplines. He amazed everyone, from the liberal arts majors to the engineers, with his knowledge of their subject matter. And his lectures were so incredibly interesting that barely a class passed during which there were not visitors who stood in the back of the classroom just to hear him lecture. The man, quite literally, played to a standing-room-only-audience. And through it all, he appeared to genuinely like his students, and treated them with respect.

And then there was Neil Postman at New York University, who introduced his students to general semantics, but also made them question some of the things about teaching, and life, that they had always accepted but never before questioned.

But then, I am reminded of another great teacher, and still another. There seems almost no end. Think about the great teachers that you have known, and think about what they did that made them great. And observe the great teachers you work with, and what they do that makes them great. Learn from them all. And even more importantly, carry on their legacy.

And, while you are at it, think about some of the less than stellar teachers you have known. What did they do that made them less than effective? What did they do that you want to be sure that you don't do?

5

COMMUNICATING EFFECTIVELY

In the midst of great joy, do not promise anyone anything.
In the midst of great anger, do not answer anyone's letter.

Chinese proverb

GETTING PARENTS ON YOUR SIDE

I've seen many, many teachers, some of them excellent teachers, deal much less than effectively with parents. That is truly unfortunate, because your students' parents can be your greatest allies—or they can cause you incredible grief.

Consider this example. Mary Smith rarely does her homework, and has consequently failed a major examination. The teacher schedules a conference with Mary's mother, and "reads her the riot act."

Teacher: "Mary is not doing her homework, and is consequently failing the class. If this continues, she will probably have to take English 2 over again next year."

Mrs. Smith apologizes for Mary's poor performance, and leaves feeling more than a little discouraged. Mary certainly hasn't been working as hard as she did last year, and she hasn't been particularly easy at home either. But still, Mrs. Smith can't help but wonder why this teacher can't get Mary to work as hard as last year's English teacher did.

Now I'm not at all suggesting that Mary's teacher is in any way responsible for Mary's poor work, or that last year's teacher was any better than he is. But I am suggesting that Mary's teacher has been less than effective in enlisting Mrs. Smith's help in getting Mary to work harder.

Think about it. In a sense, the teacher has "yelled at" Mrs. Smith because of Mary's failure to perform appropriately. Perhaps it was an outgrowth of the teacher's frustration with Mary's poor performance, or perhaps it was other pressures. But whatever the reason, the teacher has made Mrs. Smith feel more than a little defensive, and still, no better able to change Mary's attitude than the teacher is.

The secret of dealing effectively with parents is to understand their needs and capabilities, and to actively enlist their support. And it is also to understand that your students' parents want their children to succeed as much as you do—most likely even more than you do. But they may feel as powerless as you do to effect positive changes.

Now, consider how another teacher handled the very same parent conference.

Teacher: "Good morning, Mrs. Smith. I'm really happy that you were able to meet with me this morning. Mary is smart, and she is enthusiastic. But I'm concerned about her progress in class this year. She usually comes to class without having done her homework.

"This is a real problem because homework reinforces what students learn in class. Without this reinforcement, Mary failed the last major examination. If Mary did her homework, I am certain that she could easily pass her examinations.

"Perhaps we can work together to get Mary to do her homework. Would it be possible for you to check Mary's homework in the evening? That would help to impress upon her the importance of doing her homework. And I will be happy to write a short comment on her assignment every day. Let her know that you are interested in seeing my comments also.

"We both have the same goal—we both want Mary to succeed. And I am certain that by working together, we can help her to accomplish that goal.

"If there's anything that I do, please don't hesitate to let me know. And thanks, again, very much, for coming in to see me this morning."

Consider that this teacher has spent no more time than the first teacher, but this teacher has accomplished much more than the first teacher. He has:

- thanked Mrs. Smith for coming in to speak with him,
- begun by saying something positive about Mary,
- told Mrs. Smith that he and Mrs. Smith both have the same goals— that is, they both want Mary to succeed,
- explained what he will do to help,
- made a concrete proposal about how Mrs. Smith can help her daughter to do better, and
- expressed confidence that by working together they will help Mary succeed.

Of course, in this "business" there are no guarantees—it is certainly possible that Mary may not respond appropriately. But don't you agree that the second teacher is more likely to have enlisted the support of the parent, and consequently has a much greater likelihood of success than the first? And, as an added bonus, the teacher has very likely turned the parent into an ally and a supporter.

LET YOUR STUDENTS KNOW WHAT YOU EXPECT

You teach from a syllabus so you always know where you are, and where you will be going. And most likely you also have a set of expectations and classroom rules that you want your students to follow. Your syllabus, expectations, and classroom rules enable you to manage your class effectively, and to successfully cover the material that you intend to cover.

While most teachers discuss expectations and classroom rules with their students, many neglect to discuss the syllabus with them. Consequently, students are well aware of where they have been and where they are, but often don't have a clear idea of where they are going, and consequently how everything fits together.

I would like to suggest that in all but the lowest grades you present your students with a printed document at the beginning of the year that describes:

- the course outline (they don't need the detail that you include in the syllabus that you actually teach from),
- expected outcomes,
- student responsibilities,
- attendance and punctuality,
- classroom rules, and
- anything else, such as how you calculate grades, that will ensure that your students have a clear picture of what they will be learning and what you expect of them.

You can think of this document as a contract between you and your students—how you, as the teacher, will function, the outcomes that you expect your students to achieve, what you expect from your students, how you will grade them, and how you expect them to conduct themselves in your classroom.

You can use whatever style appeals to you. I have seen these kinds of statements in a very businesslike style, and I have seen them in a more casual or even humorous format. The important thing is that your students have as clear an idea of what will be happening in your classroom and what you expect of them as you do.

An added advantage of this kind of document is that on those rare occasions when an issue arises regarding, for example, a student's grade, it should be fairly easy to resolve. The student has received a clear and formal statement of your expectations, rules, and grading policies. If the student appeals your decision to an administrator, it is obvious to the administrator that you acted in a fair and reasonable manner.

LET YOUR STUDENTS' PARENTS KNOW WHAT YOU EXPECT

After you have prepared a course outline, expectations, and rules for your students, prepare a very similar document for your students' parents. Since both documents will be very similar, you should be able to prepare the second document fairly quickly and easily.

Don't give the "parent document" to your students and ask them to take it home—except in the earlier grades where you might put it in students' lunch boxes or backpacks. If you ask students to give it to their parents, very few of the documents will likely be delivered. Rather, mail it home.

In fact, you can save yourself a lot of work by giving each student a few envelopes on the first day of class. Ask them to address the envelopes to their parents and collect them. Use one now to mail your syllabus and rules home, and use the others as you need them.

Your purpose in sending the class information to your students' parents is not only to provide them with information that will help them monitor their children's work, but also to help to form a partnership with them. To this end, include a letter, like the one that follows, to introduce yourself to your students' parents, and explain why you are sending the information to them.

Dear Parent,

I would like to take this opportunity to introduce myself to you. I will be your child's teacher for the next year. I will probably spend as much time with him or her as you will—on some days, perhaps even more. And I want you to know that I will do everything that I can to help your child succeed in class.

I am sending you some information about the class—information about what we will be studying, expectations, grades, and other information that I think you will find interesting and helpful.

If you have any questions or concerns, please do not hesitate to contact me. And if necessary, I hope you will not mind if I do the same.

I look forward to a really good year.

Very best wishes,

(Your Name)

USING E-MAIL TO STAY CONNECTED

As more and more homes have computers and Internet access, e-mail is becoming a popular way of communicating with students' parents, and in some cases, even with students. I routinely give my college classes my e-mail address, and find that e-mail is an excellent way to keep in contact with them. And, it requires considerably less of my time than you might expect.

If you decide that you would like to communicate with your students and the parents via e-mail, there are a number of things that I think you should keep in mind.

1. Unless all your students' parents have access to e-mail, be sure to provide an alternative way for parents who do not have e-mail access to contact you.
2. You may not want to use your regular e-mail address for communicating with parents and/or students. Fortunately, you can obtain a free Internet-based e-mail account from any of several different sources, and use it only for your work-related communications. Two excellent free Internet-based e-mail services are: www.hotmail.com and www.yahoo.com (with Yahoo e-mail, after you go to www.yahoo.com, click on the MAIL option).
3. People see e-mail as much more immediate than regular, or "snail mail." If you decide to use e-mail as a way of communicating with your students or their parents, be sure to check your e-mail daily, and respond to messages quickly.
4. Remember that anything you write can be printed. Don't write anything that you would not want someone else to see.
5. Be careful that your words express what you want to say. Written communication is much more open to misinterpretation than oral communication. Be careful if, for example, you are joking that your words cannot be interpreted as being serious.
6. Don't ever send an e-mail message in anger, or if you aren't absolutely certain that you want to send it. You never want to be in the position of changing your mind after you've clicked the Send button and it's too late to get your message back. If you aren't sure, wait an hour before you actually send your message.

DEALING WITH AN ANGRY PARENT

It's inevitable. No matter how good your teaching skills and no matter how much you care about your students, you will occasionally encounter an angry parent. Sometimes the parent will be angry with you. Sometimes the parent will be angry with the school. And sometimes, the parent is just plain angry. But in each of these cases, one fact is inevitable—you are there, and the anger is very likely directed at you.

Occasionally, the anger may be based on an unreasonable expectation that the parent has. But just as often, it will have some basis in fact. In either case, however, it is usually best for you to try to resolve the problem rather than sending the parent to an administrator. In fact, most administrators usually insist, as they should, that parents speak to their child's teacher before they themselves become involved.

The hardest part of dealing with an angry parent is to avoid becoming emotionally involved. If you do become emotionally involved, your chances of dealing with the problem effectively, and resolving it, are practically nonexistent. So take a deep breath, and determine to yourself that you will stay calm, no matter what happens, or what the parent says.

Dealing with an angry, abusive parent.

That is not to say that you should ever accept abuse from a parent— or from anyone else, for that matter. If a parent becomes abusive, tell them that you will be very happy to listen to them, and to talk to them for as long as necessary, but that if they become abusive you will be forced to end the conversation. If you say this and the parent continues to speak to you abusively, inform them, politely but firmly, that you are sorry, but the conversation is over.

If this happens, be certain to inform your administrator, as quickly as possible, as to what has happened. There is a good chance that the parent is headed directly to the administrator's office.

Now for the other situation, dealing with an angry but non-abusive parent.

Fortunately, most parents, even if they are angry, do not become abusive. When you are confronted by an angry but non-abusive parent, the first thing you will want to do is to listen to the parent's concerns. Show the parent that you are interested in their concerns by making eye contact and asking questions that indicate your concern. Taking notes also shows that you are concerned. Often, the parent needs to talk about the problem, and needs to know that someone is interested in their concerns. In these cases, allowing him or her talk may be all that is necessary to resolve the problem. But even if it isn't, listening is still an important first step.

Assure the parent that you understand his concerns by repeating them. And also indicate that you understand his frustration. "I can certainly understand that you're unhappy that John is not being permitted to participate in the class trip. And I understand how frustrated you feel." It's really important that the parent knows that you appreciate his position, even if ultimately you are to tell him that you do not agree with it.

If the problem involves some classroom procedure, explain why you have adopted the procedure, and why you think that it is educationally sound and reasonable. Stress the fact that your objective is for the parent's child, and for all your students, to succeed, and that you feel that the procedures that you have adopted will help achieve that end.

If that doesn't work, ask the parent, very simply, but sincerely, "What would you like me to do?" If the parent's request is reasonable and you are in a position to grant it, assure him that you will be happy to comply. And if you cannot honor the parent's request, explain why you cannot.

Often, in these situations you cannot do what the parent wants because of a school or school district procedure or policy. Explain to the parent that you did not create the procedure or policy, and tell him that only the person or body that did can reverse it.

When the parent has a problem with a school or school district procedure or policy, resist the urge to defend the procedure or policy even if you agree with it. The parent is angry about a procedure or policy, and by defending it you run the very real risk that they will direct their anger—toward you. It is far better to say, "The principal instituted that procedure, and if you're really unhappy about it, it will be necessary for you to speak with him about it."

Fortunately, you will very likely encounter few angry parents. On those rare occasions when you do, remember that you will never be able to make every parent happy. But if you follow these suggestions, you should be able to deal effectively with most of the angry parents you encounter. And you will also have gone a long way to preventing those difficult situations from becoming worse.

THIS TECHNIQUE WILL WORK WONDERS

Here's an easy way to motivate your students and also to get their parents on your side. Best of all, it will work for virtually all of your students. And it will very likely work best with your most difficult students.

Make it a point to call a few parents each week to tell them about something good that their children have done in school. Consider the following telephone call.

Teacher: "Hello, is this John?"
Student: "Yes, who is this?"
Teacher: "John, this is Mr. Smith, your English teacher. May I please speak with your mother or father?"
Student: "Uh . . . what did I do?"
Teacher: "Nothing, John, but I would like to speak to your mother or father."
Student: "Maaa."
Parent: "Hello, this is Mrs. Jones."
Teacher: "Hello, Mrs. Jones, this is Mr. Smith, John's English teacher."
Parent: "What did he do now?"
Teacher: "No, no, Mrs. Smith. John didn't do anything wrong. I just called to tell you that we were discussing a really difficult topic in class today, and John not only participated, but he answered several questions correctly."

There is a really good chance that Mrs. Smith has never received a telephone call like this one.

- Imagine how it will make her feel.
- Imagine what she will tell John when she gets off the telephone.
- Imagine how it will make John feel.
- And perhaps most important, imagine how John is likely to behave in class tomorrow.

It only took five minutes of your time. And it may have been the most productive five minutes of your entire day.

Try it. You will be amazed at the results. Aren't you surprised that so few of your colleagues do it? Of course, if everyone did, it would lose some of its effectiveness. So perhaps it is best not to tell them.

PUBLIC RELATIONS—PART I

Here are two conversations that two different teachers had with non-teacher friends about their jobs.

Teacher I

Teaching is the best job in the world. I work 190 days a year, am finished working at 3:00 PM, get several long vacations every year, have great benefits, and earn a great salary.

Teacher 2

Yes, I do teach 190 days a year, and I am finished working at 3:00 PM. But I start before 8:00 AM, prepare lessons and mark papers every night at home, take courses to maintain and improve my skills, and work really hard. Yes, I receive a decent salary. But on a per hour basis, including all the extra things that my work requires, I expect that I'm paid less than many people with similar education and training, and who have similar responsibilities.

I've heard both conversations more than once—many, many times actually. Think about the effects of both conversations on the listener. In the first case, the listener thinks that teachers have a really easy job, and are definitely overpaid. In the second, the listener gains some insight into what a conscientious teacher's life is like.

I have some friends who are doctors, lawyers, and accountants, but I've never heard a doctor, lawyer, or accountant say that his job is easy or that he is overpaid. But I've heard countless teachers say exactly that.

And by doing so, they have helped to degrade the impression that the general public has of their profession.

Teaching is one of the hardest jobs I've ever had—yes, even harder than school administration. Telling people that teaching is hard work is the truth. Telling anyone anything but that is counterproductive, and makes it far less likely that the public will support smaller classes and higher teacher salaries.

PUBLIC RELATIONS—PART 2

Be alert for ways to promote your class and your school, and never, ever, miss an opportunity to do so. It's good for your students, it's good for your school, it's good for your profession, and it's good for you.

Many people think that public relations is something that you hire someone to do. While many organizations hire public relations professionals to promote their activities, some of the most effective public relations efforts are accomplished by people who work for organizations. People just like you.

And public relations doesn't necessarily involve activities on a large scale. Really effective public relations efforts are often very subtle. They don't even look like public relations. But then the best public relations usually doesn't look like public relations.

Before you think about ways to promote your class and your school, think for a moment about to whom you want to promote them. Public relations specialists understand that public relations involves a number of publics. Who are your publics?

- your students,
- their parents,
- your colleagues,
- your school administration,
- your school district administration,
- the school board,
- the community (including community members who do not have children in school),

- the media, and
- anyone else who will listen.

While some of your efforts will reach only one of these groups, some will reach many, or even all of them.

Tell your students that they are a terrific class, and most of them will rise to the occasion. Tell their parents that their children are a terrific group, and they will not only encourage them to do better, but they will become your greatest supporters.

If your class does something special, tell the school administration about it. Not only will your class look good, but you as their teacher will also look good. And if it is something really special, your administrator is likely to tell his or her administrator, because when something good happens in their school, it makes them look good. Of course, that doesn't detract from the fact that when that happens, you and your class look really good also.

A Few Words of Caution

Don't bypass your administrator and go to the central office administration with news of your success. Let your administrator bring stories of your successes to the central office administration.

And never go to the media yourself. Most school districts have someone who is responsible for all contacts with the media to prevent potential misunderstandings. More than one teacher has found himself in hot water because he made comments to the media that were subsequently misstated or misinterpreted. In fact, if someone from the media contacts you, politely direct them to your administrator for answers to their questions.

DISCIPLINE

Teaching a child not to step on a caterpillar is as valuable to the child as it is to the caterpillar.

THE TEACHER'S ROLE IN DISCIPLINE

A number of years ago I was appointed Dean of Students at a large New York City high school. The dean's job was to deal with discipline problems. It involved all kinds of problems, from relatively minor infractions such as cutting classes, to much more serious problems like assaults and drug sales. And, of course, it involved everything between those two extremes.

When the school principal appointed me dean he told me that my responsibility was to deal with problem students. He told me that he specifically did not want me to act like a psychologist or a guidance counselor. "Your job," he said, "is not to find out why a student is causing problems or to try to help him, but rather, to get him to stop."

Of course, a dean's role is different from a teacher's role. The dean often doesn't see a student until the teacher, and often the psychologist or guidance counselor, have used everything in "their bag of tricks" to try to resolve the problem.

But the principal's comments raised an important issue for me, an issue that is as important for the classroom teacher as it is for the Dean of Students. And, I think, it is critical that teachers consider this issue before problems occur. Is your role to try to help a problem student, or is it to keep him from interfering with the education of the other students in your class? That's a big question. What do you think?

The answer, I think, is both of these. Certainly, you want to try to help every student in your class to succeed. But when an individual student's behavior interferes with the learning of other students, you have an even more compelling reason to stop the disruptive behavior as quickly as possible.

Serious Situations

Let's deal with the most obvious problem first, the situation in which you believe that a student is a danger to himself or to other students in your class. This one is a "no brainer." You need to notify the school administration as quickly as possible. And if the situation presents an immediate danger, you need to send another student to obtain the assistance of an administrator immediately. In this case, be certain that the student tells the administrator that you have an emergency in your classroom.

Then, as soon as possible after the student has been removed from your classroom it is important that you write an unemotional, factual description of exactly what has happened and what your concerns are. Be sure to indicate the date and time that the incident occurred, and all other pertinent details.

And above all, be certain that your narrative is unemotional and factual. "On February 1, at 9:00 AM, John picked up a chair and began to swing it in the proximity of several other students. I took the chair from him, and called for administrative support. Mr. Smith, the Assistant Principal, removed John from the classroom."

Do not write, "John has serious emotional problems and could kill someone." That statement is completely subjective. Describe what has happened, and let the reader draw conclusions about John's emotional state from your factual statement.

Less Serious Situations

With less serious problems, your role, and the question of when to seek administrative support, is less clear-cut. But fortunately, in these situations, you have more time to decide how to best proceed. Your best course of action is usually to try to work with the student to try to resolve the problem.

Again, it will be a good idea to keep a brief written record of your conversations with the student. You don't need to write anything extensive—just a few short comments will be sufficient. As with more serious problems, record the date and times of your conversations, and a brief summary of your comments to the student and his responses. And also, as in the case of more serious situations, be certain that your comments are factual and unemotional. Do not say, for example, "John was surly and disrespectful." It is much better to indicate exactly what you said, and what he responded.

The reason for your written record is to enable you to remember what both you and the student have said. However, a written record has the potential of serving two additional purposes:

1. If at some point you feel that it will be advantageous to enlist the support of the guidance counselor, school social worker, or school psychologist, your notes will provide valuable insights to these staff members.
2. Should the problems escalate to the point where you need to refer the student to the school administration for disciplinary support, your notes will very specifically indicate the nature of the problem, and the steps that you have taken in your attempt to resolve it.

Dealing with discipline problems is never easy, and it is never fun. But the need to deal with an occasional discipline problem is an unavoidable part of the job. When discipline problems arise, deal with them in a decisive, reasonable, and unemotional way, you will be able to get past them quickly, and to get on with the real job that they hired you for.

BEHAVIOR AND NEEDS

A student misbehaves in your class. You encourage him . . . you discipline him . . . you call his parents . . . perhaps you even have him suspended from class for a few days. But the problems persist unabated.

What's going on here? The answer is most likely that somehow, on some level, the student's unacceptable behavior is meeting his needs. There are a lot of possible reasons for this. Perhaps the student is seeking attention from his parents or teachers, and for him, even negative attention is preferable to no attention at all. Or perhaps his parents are involved in an angry divorce, in the midst of which he feels powerless—or angry.

Of course, there are countless possibilities. But the bottom line, again, is that the student's behavior is somehow meeting his needs. The question, of course, is what can you do? The answer is that you want to try to discover the cause of the student's unacceptable behavior. That may or may not be possible. But whether it is possible to discover the cause of the student's unacceptable behavior or not, your goal is to try to substitute some socially acceptable behavior for the student's inappropriate behavior.

Start by spending some private time with the student. You may want to ask him directly why he is misbehaving in your class. But understand that it is most likely that he doesn't understand anything about the dynamics of his behavior. It will probably be more effective to just try to get him to talk about what is going on in his life. Who does he live with? What is his family like? What does he like to do? What does he hope to do after he finishes school?

Of course, you will say, "But I'm not a psychologist. How can I make sense of what he tells me?" Then answer is that you certainly are not a psychologist, and you certainly are not expected to be able to determine what it all means. What you are trying to do is to show the student that you are interested in him as a person—that he is more than just a student in a class. And you are also trying to develop a relationship with him. It usually works. And in the course of your conversations, you may find out something important that will help you understand why he is acting as he is.

Another advantage of your conversations with the student is that they give the student an opportunity to interact with, and have a relationship with, a stable adult. Certainly, his parents may be stable, but they may just as likely not be. If the student's parents are unstable, interacting with you can be a stabilizing influence in his life. As an added advantage, you can serve as a good role model for him.

Of course, if necessary you will also be able to discuss what you have learned about the student with the school guidance counselor or the school district psychologist. Perhaps the counselor or psychologist can help to shed some additional light on the student's problem, and how to best deal with it. But whatever help the counselor or psychologist can be, if you can develop a relationship with the student you will have gone a long way toward helping him to behave more appropriately and less self-destructively.

IRRATIONAL BEHAVIOR

Occasionally, in spite of all the time that you spend trying to understand and help a student, he will continue to act inappropriately. In fact, his behavior may be so odd as to defy comprehension—by you, and by the school counselor and psychologist. The behavior is, simply put, irrational.

Fortunately, irrational behavior is relatively rare. But it does occur, and in the course of your career you are certain to come across instances of irrational behavior from time to time. So it is important that you understand the nature of irrational behavior and how to deal with it when you encounter it.

A number of years ago, I found myself dealing with a truly bizarre young lady. Much as I tried to understand her, I could not determine why she was acting the way she was. All my attempts to work with her, to get to know her, and to get her to behave acceptably were met with failure.

I mentioned my frustration with this student to a psychiatrist friend of mine. He said, quite simply, "Her behavior is irrational."

"But," I continued, "I can't understand why she is doing the things that she is doing."

He replied, "The nature of irrational behavior is that it doesn't make sense. So it should be obvious that irrational behavior defies explanation. And rational attempts at dealing with irrational behavior are almost always futile."

So what do you do when you encounter irrational behavior? The answer is that it depends on the particular behavior. A considerable number of people act irrationally in some area of their lives. A young man washes his hands 20 or 30 times each day. And a young woman goes out with a succession of men, each of whom treats her badly. Obviously, both behaviors are irrational. But they don't impact on your classroom. However, when a student's irrational behavior significantly impacts on the functioning of your classroom, you need to become more proactive. And in this kind of situation, that means notifying the school administration and support staff.

Above all, when you encounter irrational behavior and see it as such, it is important for you to remember that irrational behavior doesn't make sense, and that it doesn't respond to rational intervention. Obviously, you will need to involve the school counselor or psychologist. And you will most likely also need to involve the school administration. And above all, you need to understand that sometimes you will be powerless to understand why a student is behaving as he is, or to effect a positive change.

DISCIPLINE AND EXPECTATIONS

Discipline problems occur everywhere—in every school and at every academic level. Certainly, discipline problems are more common in some schools than in others. And certainly, too, they are much more common at some academic levels. But rest assured that no classroom is immune. I have seen discipline problems in pre-school classes, and I have seen them in graduate university classes.

But the fact that discipline problems are, to some degree, inevitable does not mean that there is nothing that you can do to prevent many of them from occurring. There are effective ways of dealing with virtually every imaginable problem.

Your demeanor and attitude are a significant factor in determining to what degree discipline problems will occur in your classroom. I firmly believe that if you treat your students courteously and with respect, and expect that they will treat you, and each other, in the same way, most potential problems will never occur.

At some levels and in some schools, of course, that is fairly easy to do. Say, "please" and "thank you," and mean it. When you ask a student a question, say, "Will you please explain to the class . . . ?" And after the explanation, say, "Thank you for sharing that with us." You will be amazed at how much more positive your students will be, and how contagious your courtesy, and theirs, will become.

Of course, in some places and with some students you will have to work much harder to engender courtesy in your classroom. In these cases you may find it helpful to explain the "rules" to your students on the very first day of class. And you may find it necessary to repeat them from time to time, remembering, of course, that your actions will be as important as your words.

The more difficult the environment, the more you will have to work at it. Consider the following, with some modification.

"Good morning. My name is Mr. Smith, and we're going to be studying world history together this year. But before we begin, I would like to tell you how we're going interact in this room.

"I promise that I will always treat you with respect. If you believe that I have been less than respectful to you, I would expect that you will talk to me about it—privately, and after class. And if I believe that you have been less than respectful to another student or to me, I will talk to you about it—also privately, and after class."

Remember that this will not work if you do not treat your students, all of your students, with respect. And it will not work if you do not insist that they treat you and each other similarly. And remember too that for some period of time you may have to remind your students, at least occasionally, that "courtesy is spoken here." But rest assured that eventually they will no longer need to be reminded. As a bonus, your classroom will become a nicer place for your students, and for you. As an added bonus, you will find that your job is actually much easier.

MINOR INFRACTIONS

Despite your insistence on courtesy and respect, from time to time a student will act out in class. It's inevitable. What do you do? Of course, how you respond to a problem depends on the nature of the problem. The more serious and overt the problem, the more significant must be your response.

Let's begin with a minor infraction. Suppose two students are carrying on a conversation during your lesson. Often a disapproving glance will be all that is needed. And if "The Glance" works, follow it with a gentle smile. Or if they don't respond to your glance, a simple, "Please," followed by a smile and, "Thanks." Just be sure that the "Please" is sincere, that it does not sound sarcastic, and that the smile and the "Thank you" are also genuine.

It's actually just a little harder than it sounds. Actors and actresses practice their lines, often many times, until they can get them to convey exactly the feeling they want. So practice "The Glance," your "Please," and your "Thank you" in front of a mirror to be sure that they convey the precise meaning that you want them to. There are no Academy Awards here, but you are sure to find that the time you have spent "rehearsing" will have been very well spent.

MORE SERIOUS INFRACTIONS

Sometimes a student will do something that is more serious or overt. Or sometimes, the student's behavior will be disruptive to the class, and "The Glance," or "Please," just won't work. Obviously, in these cases you need to become more proactive—but still, I maintain, you can do it in a courteous and respectful way.

Your major consideration, in every situation, should be to avoid a direct confrontation with a student at all costs. Think of it this way. Both you and the student have an audience—the students in your classroom. If the student feels that he is losing face in front of his peers, he is likely to do whatever he feels is necessary to prevent that from happening. If he becomes defiant by refusing to follow directions, cursing at you, or walking out of the room when you have told him to sit down, there is no question but that he has, in a sense, won. And if he wins, obviously, you have lost.

Of course, you may ultimately win—by, say, having the student disciplined by the school administrator, suspended from school, or even transferred to another class. But at the moment that the incident is occurring you are likely to appear to everyone present to have lost control.

Your best bet in these situations is to say, "Please see me after class." You want to sound serious and in control, but not confrontational or threatening.

If the situation absolutely won't wait, you can walk to the door and ask the student to talk to you in the hallway. Out of sight of the students in the class, and without an audience, he is much less likely to become defiant. But even if he does, no one in the class will be aware of what has happened. And if you absolutely cannot have the student return to the classroom, you can send him to the office with instructions to wait for you there.

The worst-case scenario is that despite your best efforts a student becomes openly defiant. On these rare occasions, one very effective technique is to stop teaching, sit down at your desk, and begin to write down what the student is saying. When he realizes what you are doing, he will usually stop. At that point, ask the student, in a firm but calm voice, to see you after the class has ended.

Of course, if a student is completely out of control, your only option may be to send another student for administrative support. It certainly works, but it is something that you want to do very infrequently. Unless the student is completely out of control, it may appear to your class, and possibly the school administration as well, that you were unable to control your class.

FIGHTS

Depending on the school you work in, fights may be a rare occurrence, or they may occur on a daily basis. In either case, it is important to know how you will react to a fight before you are confronted with a situation in which you have to deal with one.

But first, I think it is important for you to understand why fights occur. Most fights occur for one of the following reasons:

- One student is angry with another. That is, one student wants to fight, and most likely the other does not.

- Two students are angry at each other. Both students may want to fight. But it is just as likely that only one student wants to fight.
- One student feels that he has been publicly embarrassed by another, and needs to save face. Again, one student wants to fight— or more likely, feels that he must do something to protect his reputation. Most likely, the other student does not want to fight.
- Two students feel that they have been publicly embarrassed by each other, and both feel that they need to "save face." Two students feel that they need to act to protect their reputations. One or both may feel that fighting is a way to achieve this.
- A crowd of students surrounds two angry students, making it difficult for them not to fight. The presence of onlookers encourages two students to fight, and it also makes it harder for the combatants to stop fighting even though both may be eager to stop. In fact, in most situations the fight is at least partly a result of encouragement from onlookers.

Keep in mind that in most instances one student, or even both students, do not want to be fighting. This usually makes it easier to stop a fight. However, it does not mean that stopping a fight is necessarily easy, or that by doing so that you are not risking your own safety.

Wherever you work and whatever you teach, someday you will be confronted by two or more students who are fighting. Before you are confronted by this situation, assess your own capabilities. Obviously, a petite young woman is not likely to be able to respond in the same way as a burly physical education teacher.

In any case, it is important that the fighting stop as quickly as possible. The longer the fight continues, the more likely that one or both of the combatants will be seriously injured. While not as serious as the danger that one or more students will become seriously injured, it is also important to understand that the failure to act quickly can open the school district, and also the teacher, to possible legal liability.

If you feel that you have the presence to stop a fight, make a very forceful statement, in your most imposing voice. Say something like, "Stop that right now, and both of you come with me!" In many cases, that will be all that is necessary. As the students hesitate, take each firmly by one arm and bring them to another location, preferably an administrative office.

But if you don't feel that you have the presence to stop a fight, do not intervene physically. You do not want to risk your own safety. Rather, summon help immediately.

As a high school Dean of Students, I frequently had to break up fights. And even more often, I had to deal with students who had been fighting. The following is how I dealt with these situations:

1. I immediately situated both students in separate locations, and informed both that they were suspended for fighting. Obviously, two students who are separated cannot fight. And by suspending the students, I informed them, and other students as well, in very real terms, that if you fight in school you will be suspended.

2. I instructed each student to provide me with a written statement as to what had happened. This gave both students a chance to calm down. And the written statements helped me determine what had caused the fight and how difficult it would be to prevent a recurrence.

3. After reading both statements, I met with one student to discuss with him his version of what had happened. This gave me an opportunity to gain additional information about what had happened. And since I had read both students' written accounts of the incident, I was in a better position to discuss the problem with the student.

4. I then met with the second student, and had a similar discussion with him.

5. If I felt that the situation was sufficiently defused, I brought both students together, and hopefully was able to help them to work out their differences.

6. The students were not permitted to return to classes, at the very least, until the next day.

7. If one student was not responsible for the fight, I allowed him to return to class on the following day. In most cases, I did not allow the student who appeared to have been responsible for having started the fight to return to class for an additional day or two.

Students needed to know the seriousness of what had happened, and that it would not be tolerated.

8. When students were allowed to return to class, they had to be accompanied to school by a parent. I had to be sure that the students' parents were aware of what had happened, and of the seriousness of the infraction, and also that they knew that the school was committed to the safety of their child, and all children.

DRUG ABUSE

Times are bad.
Children no longer obey their parents,
and everyone is writing a book.

> Marcus Tullius Cicero (orator and writer, 106–43 BC)

HOW TO TELL IF A STUDENT IS USING DRUGS

There is no question that drug abuse by young people is a major problem in schools and communities almost everywhere. In fact, in some areas it is not uncommon to see indications of drug abuse even in the
lower grades. And when you consider alcohol as the very potent drug
that it undeniably is, drug abuse among young people is, in most areas,
at epidemic proportions. Unless you teach very young children, as a
teacher you cannot ignore the fact that at least some of your students
may be abusing drugs and alcohol.

The first concern about drug abuse that most teachers have, and a
concern which is shared by most parents, is how to tell if a young person is using drugs. There are certainly physical signs that an individual
may be using drugs. The following are the major symptoms of the most
commonly abused drugs:

- **Marijuana**
  Reddened whites of eyes
  Distinctive odor on clothing
- **Stimulants**—amphetamines, cocaine, crack, others
  Dilated pupils
  Hyperactivity
- **Depressants**—barbiturates, others
  Slurred speech
  Appearance like alcohol intoxication, but without the distinctive odor of alcohol
- **Narcotics**—heroin, others
  Constricted pupils of eyes
  Drowsiness and slurred speech
- **Hallucinogens**
  Dilated pupils of eyes
  Mood changes and distorted senses

However, you should not assume that you can use this list to determine whether a student is under the influence of a particular drug, or any drug at all. Even trained drug abuse workers and medical personnel often cannot be certain without a blood or urine test.

So how can you tell if a student is under the influence of drugs? The answer is that you cannot—that is, you cannot tell with absolute certainty. But that is not to suggest that there is nothing that you can do. What you can do is to be aware of short and long-term changes in a student's appearance and behavior. These changes may indicate drug abuse. To this end, ask yourself the following questions:

- Has the student's personality changed? Has he become unexpectedly withdrawn or outgoing?
- Are there sudden changes in his work habits or school attendance?
- Has the student's physical appearance deteriorated significantly?
- Has the student's attitude changed?
- Is the student associating with different students than he formerly did, particularly students who are suspected of being drug abusers?
- Is the student wearing some inappropriate clothing, particularly sunglasses indoors or long sleeved shirts or blouses during warm weather?

But, you say, these changes may not indicate drug abuse at all. Everyone knows that young people, and particularly adolescents, are mercurial. While that is certainly correct, it does not at all indicate that the situation is hopeless. Remember that you are looking for significant changes in a student's appearance and behavior. Certainly, these kinds of changes may indicate drug abuse. But they may also indicate possible emotional difficulties. And, they may indicate nothing more than normal adolescent behavior.

WHAT SHOULD YOU DO IF YOU SUSPECT THAT A STUDENT IS USING DRUGS?

OK, so a student in your class is exhibiting some of the signs that suggest that he may be using drugs. What should you do?

There are a few things that you should definitely do in this situation. But before we discuss them, you should be aware of the one thing that you should definitely not do. It is really important that you do not suggest to the student, or to his parents, that you believe that he is using drugs—even if you are relatively certain that he is.

Remember, all you know for certain is that the student does not look the way he normally does. So ask him, directly, if he is alright. Depending on how he appears to you, you may decide to send him to the school nurse. Or you may allow him to remain in your class, but talk to the nurse about your concerns as soon as your class has ended.

If you send the student to the nurse, send him with another student to ensure that he arrives safely. And also send the nurse a note indicating that the student does not appear to be well. Indicate, also, that you will come to the nurse's office as soon as you are free, and indicate when that will be.

Whether you send the student to the school nurse or allow him to remain in your class, at your first opportunity be certain to share your concerns about the student with the school nurse. I would strongly suggest that you not indicate that you are referring the student because he is using drugs. Rather, be completely factual. Indicate that the student does not appear to be well, and be specific about how the student appears to be unwell. And also, and this is really important, indicate how the student is different from the way that he normally appears and behaves. The nurse will not know, for example, that a student who is very drowsy, or hyperactive, or argumentative is not generally drowsy, or hyperactive, or argumentative.

Of course, you can suggest to the school nurse, privately, that you suspect the possibility of drug abuse. But do not state unequivocally that that is the case. It is far better to say, for example, "John is usually wide awake in class, but today he has been falling asleep at his desk. He indicated to me that he slept well last night. Of course, he might just be very tired, but I wonder whether drugs might be involved."

Most likely, after examining the student the school nurse will meet with the student's parents, and will discuss his condition with them. If you are asked to be present at that meeting, again, do not suggest that you suspect drug abuse. Indicate only that the student did not appear to be well in your class, and that you are concerned about his well being.

Many schools have a specific procedure for the school nurse to follow in these kinds of situations. One very good procedure is to require the student's parents to have their child seen by a doctor, and to require that they provide medical verification to the school the child is well enough to return to school. If there is an indication of drug abuse, the doctor will be in a position to diagnose it definitively, and to recommend options for treatment.

TEACHING STUDENTS ABOUT DRUG ABUSE

Can schools do anything to teach students not to become involved with drugs? The answer is a qualified, "Yes."

Many people believe that schools can and should be involved in teaching students about the dangers of drug abuse. But many schools have policies regarding whether drug abuse education is to take place, and if it is, who is designated to do it. Obviously, if your school does not want drug abuse education to take place, or if it has designated someone other than you to do it, you must accede to their wishes.

School personnel who are going to teach young people about drug abuse should be very knowledgeable about the subject. And they should be particularly aware of the reasons that some young people become involved with drugs. Actually, there are only a few basic reasons:

- **Illicit Drugs Are Available.** Obviously, if drugs are not available, students cannot experiment with, or use, them.
- **Curiosity.** Students hear about drugs at school, in their neighborhood, on television and on the radio, and in the movies. With all this exposure to the subject, some students will be curious enough to want to see for themselves what all the talk is about.
- **Peer Pressure.** Some students are motivated to experiment with drugs because in their immediate environment, it is seen as "cool."

Availability of Drugs

Contrary to what many people believe, "drug pushers" very rarely force drugs on anyone who is not willing and interested in using them. In fact, most dealers don't even solicit people who are not already using drugs. Dealers are easily identifiable in the community, and people who want to buy drugs generally come to them rather than the other way around.

Obviously, there is little that you can do about the availability of illicit drugs in or near your school. The best that you can do in this regard, if you have specific information about where drugs are being sold or who is selling them, is to report what you know to the school administration, who will then, most likely, report the information to the police.

Curiosity

Dealing with curiosity about drugs is certainly part of a prevention program. To this extent, it is helpful to provide students with factual information about the nature of drugs that are commonly abused, and also, the risks involved in experimenting with them. But it is equally important to avoid presenting students with incorrect information. If they find that you have provided them with incorrect information, you will have lost your credibility and they will obtain their information elsewhere.

It is also important, I think, not to resort to "scare tactics." Scare tactics have had a minimal impact on drinking and driving, and on promiscuous sex. While students should have information about the dangers of using illicit drugs, it is unlikely that trying to frighten young people about the dangers of drug abuse will be any more effective.

Peer Pressure

Dealing with the peer pressure issue is probably the area in which schools can have the greatest impact on drug abuse. Schools can do this in two major ways.

1. Schools can encourage, and make available, a wide variety of supervised, extracurricular activities for students. The greater the number of appropriate activities that young people are involved in, and the more that they are involved with other non-drug-using students, the less likely it is that they will feel pressured into experimenting with drugs.

2. Schools can teach students acceptable ways of saying "no" to drugs. This can be a particularly effective activity, but it requires careful research, planning, and teacher training. It generally involves assigning students to directed groups in which they discuss and role play situations involving peer pressure to experiment with drugs, and learn acceptable but face-saving ways of saying "no."
   For example, students may be presented with the following scenario: You pass a group of people in a park, who are passing around a "joint." One of the young people knows you, and invites you to join them. "Hey, try it," someone says. "It's cool." You want to say, "No," but you don't want to appear uncool. What do you say? There will most likely be at least as many ways to say "no" as there are students in your classroom. And the more solutions your students hear, the more effective responses that they will have added to their repertoires.

DRUG SALES IN SCHOOLS

If a school has any drug abuse problem at all, it almost certainly has some sales taking place on school grounds. Some sales involve one student selling a very small quantity of drugs to another, but others may involve more substantial quantities. In any case, it is important for the school to do whatever it can to prevent drug sales from taking place in the school and on the school grounds.

The first step in this direction is to inform all students, and all students' parents, that any student who brings drugs to school, and particularly anyone who sells drugs, will be punished. Specifically, the police will be called. Period!

In regard to the possession of drugs on the school campus, schools may have greater latitude than even the police. While I am not suggesting that schools indiscriminately search students' lockers, schools in many locations have the legal right to do so.

Before a police officer searches someone's person or property, he must have "reasonable cause" to believe that a crime has been committed. That is, a police officer cannot indiscriminately perform a search unless he has a specific reason to believe that a crime has been committed. And if a police officer exceeds his authority in this regard, the search will be considered illegal and any evidence that was acquired as a result of the illegal search will be inadmissible in court.

Unlike the police, school officials serve in loco parentis (in place of the parents). In many localities, this allows school officials to search students without "reasonable cause," and if contraband is discovered, it is admissible in court. Less commonly, in some other jurisdictions the courts have ruled such searches illegal. Your school administration should be aware of the law in your community.

I am not at all suggesting that if school officials in your area have the legal right to indiscriminately search students or their lockers for illicit drugs that they do so—that is an issue for each school district to decide, consistent with local laws and local sentiment. All that I am saying is that in many places it is permissible. Of course, the school is not so much interested in arresting students as it is in preventing them from bringing drugs and other inappropriate items to school.

When I was the Dean of Students in a large city high school, on quite a number of occasions I encountered students with drugs—occasionally quantities that would lead one to believe that there was the intent to sell them. On those occasions, I called the police and the students were advised of their rights and arrested.

When there has been an arrest for the possession or sale of drugs in the school, it is my opinion that it is important that other students are aware of what has happened. Generally, a school administrator makes an announcement on the school public address system the following morning, indicating that a (nameless) student was apprehended in school with drugs, and was arrested.

A more controversial technique that some schools use is to have the student arrested, and escorted out of the school building by a police officer, in handcuffs, and in plain view of other students—a very visible deterrent to other students.

In any event, it is essential that schools have clear-cut policies regarding the possession and sale of drugs on school property, and well-defined procedures for dealing with situations long before an incident occurs. And it is equally important that staff members, students, and students' parents are also familiar with the school's policies in this regard.

8

WORKING WITH YOUR COLLEAGUES

It is one of the most beautiful compensations of this life that no man can sincerely try to help another without helping himself.

Ralph Waldo Emerson

THE FACULTY ROOM

A few years ago, I was working for a college that was running a program at a university in China. At one point, I was asked to go to China to deliver a few lectures, and also to conduct some negotiations there for the college.

I wasn't really enthusiastic about making the trip. While the opportunity to visit China was appealing, in my experience business travel has rarely been as much fun or as interesting as it sounds. And while the school I would be visiting was a major university and was located in a city, conditions were far from modern and not nearly as sanitary as they are here in the United States. Added to that was the fact that the trip involved a seventeen-hour flight to Beijing, and then a six-hour drive from the airport to the campus.

I could have said, "No, I don't want to go," and the college would not have objected. But there were some problems with the program, and my trip would go a long way toward helping to resolve them.

My son is a young teacher. He's bright, enthusiastic, and he works really hard. As you can imagine, we've spent many hours talking "shop." When I returned from China, we spent more than a few hours discussing my trip. My son knew that I hadn't wanted to go to China, and at some point he asked, "If you didn't want to go, why did you agree to do it?"

I explained that, "The college had a problem with the program they were running at the Chinese university, and that by going I was able to help resolve it."

My son said, "I can tell you that none of the teachers in the faculty room in my school would have done what you did."

I answered that, "In most situations, there is no single right thing to do," and that, "Everyone needs to do what is right for them. For me, the right thing to do was to go to China."

Not long afterward, I mentioned the conversation that I had had with my son to a friend of mine, a successful college administrator. I mentioned to him what my son had said about the teachers in the faculty room.

Almost without thinking, he said, "That's why they're still in the faculty room, and you're a college administrator."

That is not to say that being a teacher is somehow less important than being an administrator—at least I don't think that it is. But my "way" has been right for me, and my decisions have afforded me a considerable measure of success in my career.

But it is also important, really important I think, to understand the goals and needs of the organization that one works for, and so long as those goals are not illegal or immoral, to work in a way that is consistent with those goals and that helps the organization to achieve them. If you do this, you cannot help but increase the level of success that you achieve as a member of the organization.

FACULTY DRESS

Early in my teaching career, the school I worked for had a de facto dress code for teachers. Male teachers had to wear ties and jackets, and while mustaches were permitted, beards were not. Female teachers were not allowed to wear slacks to work, even on the coldest winter days.

At the beginning of the school year, teachers reported one day before students for a day of meetings, and to prepare their classrooms for the first day of school. At the faculty meeting that day, I remember the principal asking one teacher to stand. He said, "I want everyone to see the beard that Matt grew this summer—because it isn't going to be there tomorrow." And, there was no question that Matt was going to shave the beard before the first day of classes.

One day I came to work during a major snowstorm. I walked about two miles to a main road on which I was able to take a bus, which left me off about a mile from the school. That day, I wore a ski jacket over a shirt and tie. Many teachers were unable to report to work at all. When I arrived at school, the principal, who was standing by the time clock, was visibly upset that I was not wearing a conventional suit or sports jacket.

Those days are obviously long gone, and the working atmosphere in schools has changed dramatically. In most schools, teacher dress codes are non-existent, or at least they are vastly less restrictive than they were formerly. While most teachers in most schools dress similarly to the way office workers dress, some teachers in some schools look reasonably unkempt. On occasion, I've even seen a teacher in work boots and torn jeans.

Does a teacher's dress affect the learning that takes place in his classroom? Certainly there are those who believe that it does. And there are those who believe, equally fervently, that it does not.

My personal opinion is that the way a teacher dresses does have an impact on the learning that takes place in his classroom. That is not to say that I think that male teachers should be required to wear ties and jackets and that female teachers must wear suits, dresses, or skirts and blouses. But I think that "neat and clean" gives students the impression that what is taking place is serious and important. It also instills in them the notion that one dresses a certain way when one goes to work.

However, another advantage of dressing in a more "professional" manner is that it makes it more likely that the community will see its teachers as professionals. And the more that a community perceives its teachers as professionals, the more support it generally affords them.

SUPPORTING YOUR COLLEAGUES

In some businesses, if someone does a less than adequate job everyone else looks better by comparison. For example, if an inadequate mechanic works on my car, your mechanic looks even better than he otherwise would. However, this is generally not the case in schools. If one teacher is less than capable, many parents will see teachers in general as being less than capable. It may not be fair, but that's the way it often is.

With this in mind, all teachers gain by supporting each other. Share good techniques and good lessons with your colleagues, and they are very likely to reciprocate. If you feel that another teacher is having problems, consider offering to help. And in particular, if you have the urge to "put down" another teacher, especially to parents or other outsiders, resist it. We're all in this together. And if one of us looks good, we all look good—or at least better than we otherwise would have.

SOMETIMES YOU JUST HAVE TO WALK AWAY

Some teachers, and of course some people in all walks of life, like to argue. The problem is that arguments are rarely productive. Worse, they often cause problems.

When I was a high school counselor, I learned a lot about college financial aid, and was considered a local expert on the subject. As you can imagine, many students and parents, and even teachers and administrators, came to me for help with their financial aid forms.

One day a teacher came to my office to ask for help with his son's financial aid forms. The teacher told me that although his son was living with him, he didn't give his son any money and didn't want his income considered in determining his son's eligibility for financial aid. I explained to him that his son didn't meet the established criteria for "financial independence."

"But you don't understand," he said, "I don't give him any money."

I replied, "I do understand, John, but I'm just answering your question. I didn't make the rules"

"But you don't understand," he continued. "You aren't being fair."

Again I told him, "John, the rules have been established by an act of Congress. I didn't create them, I'm just telling you what they are."

Not to be deterred by the facts, John was actually becoming angry at me. He repeated, "But you aren't being fair."

Of course, John wasn't hearing me. And no matter how many times I explained the situation, he wasn't going to hear me. Obviously, arguing with him would have been pointless. I said, simply, "I'm sorry John, but the conversation is over." And I walked away.

Sometimes you win, and sometimes you lose. And sometimes, it's best to just walk away.

DEALING WITH AN ANGRY TEACHER—PART I

Some of your students arrive in your class late every day. When you ask them what the problem is, they tell you that their math teacher always keeps them late. He tells them that, "Math is much more important than English." Of course, it creates a problem for you. You start your lesson, and then you have to repeat the beginning when these students arrive. Or, it can be any one of a thousand other problems. What to do?

The first thing is what you should not do. Be absolutely certain that you do not take it out on the students—it certainly isn't their fault that their math teacher is keeping them late. And don't ask them to talk to the teacher, or to try to resolve the problem in any other way. The teacher knows that he is sending the students to your class late. There would be no advantage to putting your students in the middle of a difficult situation, a situation that they are much less able to deal with than you are.

I would also suggest that you not attempt to seek help from an administrator for relatively minor problems with other staff members—at least not until you have exhausted all your other options. My suggestion in a situation like this one would be to try to talk to the teacher, preferably alone. Ask him if you and he can sit down and talk about the problem privately. If you have trouble setting up a meeting with the teacher, send him a note asking if you can both meet privately at some mutually convenient time and place.

When you do meet, try to do it in a casual, friendly place—say over a cup of coffee. Try to explain the problem that you are experiencing. But don't become emotional, and don't let the discussion escalate into an argument. And even though you may be certain that you are one hundred percent right, if the other teacher is unyielding, see if you can find a mutually acceptable compromise. A fifty-percent compromise is far better than zero resolution.

If the teacher will not meet with you, or is unyielding, you need to decide if the issue is worth pursuing. If you are certain that it is, try to enlist the assistance of a school counselor, union or teachers' association representative, or lead teacher. If all else fails, then ask the school principal for assistance. You certainly don't want to feel that you and your students are being taken advantage of. But remember that many problems that seem really important today will seem much less important a week or a month from now.

DEALING WITH AN ANGRY TEACHER—PART 2

Dealing with a relatively minor problem with another teacher may be difficult. But dealing with a more overt problem is always difficult—much more difficult. And it is also much more likely to require administrative support.

Consider the following scenario. One of your students was absent from your class on the day of an important exam. His mother has requested that you give him an opportunity to make up the exam within the next few days so that his report card mark will not be affected. You reschedule the exam for tomorrow afternoon. The student tells you that he is on the wrestling team and is scheduled to participate in a wrestling meet tomorrow afternoon. But grades are due the following day. So you tell him that if he wants to take the examination before grades are entered he must take it tomorrow afternoon.

The following afternoon the student and a few other students are taking the examination in your classroom when the wrestling coach arrives at your classroom door. He is verbally abusive to you within earshot of your students. He yells, "You are in big trouble," and that, "You had better watch your step."

You close the door to avoid a direct confrontation with the teacher, and so that the students will not be a party to his tirade. But you have been put in a very difficult situation, and worse, in front of a group of students. You feel, justifiably, that you cannot ignore what has happened. What should you do?

I would agree that this is the kind of situation that you most likely must address, lest it escalate. And it is also the kind of situation that I do not think you can resolve yourself. A teacher who acts unprofessionally and abusively is not likely, I think, to discuss the issue reasonably, and is also unlikely to be amenable to a reasonable resolution. In most cases like this one, you will need help. And in most cases, you will need that help from your administrator.

My suggestion is that the first thing you should do is write down exactly what has happened. Indicate the date and time, and the names of the students who were in your classroom. And indicate, to the best of your ability, exactly what the teacher said. I would then suggest that you meet with the school principal or administrator as soon as possible after the event, explaining what has happened and giving him a copy of your narrative. If the principal is not eager to become involved, you might explain why you feel that the problem is so serious, and that your concern is that if it is not resolved that it may well recur, or even escalate.

In most cases, the school principal will arrange a meeting with you and the other teacher. The resolution you want is an understanding that a similar incident will never recur. In an ideal world, you would get a sincere apology. But in the real world, that may not happen. If you do not get an apology, let it go. Your major objective, after all, is to do whatever you can to prevent a recurrence of the problem, and to undo any damage that may have been done.

A FEW WORDS ABOUT
ADMINISTRATORS

To know the road ahead, ask those coming back.

Chinese proverb

WHAT THEY SAY AND WHAT THEY MEAN

Years ago when I was the Dean of Students at a New York City high
school, the principal told me that he did not want me to get information
about one student from another. "Tattling," he told me, "is not educationally sound."

Then, one day a visiting opera company performed at the school. It was
not until after they had left that they realized that the jacket from one of
their costumes was missing. The opera company immediately called the
Board of Education, who as you can imagine, immediately called the principal. He, in turn, called me. Of course, everyone wanted the jacket returned immediately—if not sooner.

I assumed that at least some of the students on the "stage crew" knew
who had taken the jacket. But I had been enjoined not to get information
about one student from another. What to do? Of course, I interviewed
the students on the stage crew, individually, and got the jacket back in

fairly short order. The principal was overjoyed. He never asked how I got the jacket back. And since I never brought the subject up, he never knew.

The point is that usually, when your supervisors tell you what they want you to do, that is what they want you to do. But sometimes, it isn't. "We want you to teach the course material," they may say, "not to prepare students to pass the state exam." But you know that they will be really unhappy if your students do not do well on the state exam.

Always listen carefully to what your supervisors tell you to do. But understand that occasionally what they say may not be what they really mean. Always try to discover what your supervisors really want you to do, and do that, even if it conflicts with what they have said. But be discreet—don't talk about it.

OBSERVATIONS AND EVALUATIONS

All schools have provisions for conducting formal teacher observations, and for evaluating teachers. Frequently, supervisors observe new teachers much more often than their more seasoned counterparts. But observations and evaluations are a part of life for all teachers.

Observations

Observations involve a supervisor or administrator visiting your class, and may be informal or formal. An informal observation may be announced or unannounced—that is, you may or may not know that the administrator is planning to visit your class in advance. And with informal observations, the administrator will usually be in your classroom for a relatively short period of time. A formal observation, on the other hand, is usually announced (although some administrators do not announce formal observations), and almost always involves the administrator's watching you teach an entire lesson or topic.

Informal observations are usually followed by an informal discussion of the lesson. But formal observations usually involve the preparation of a written observation report and a formal conference in which the observer discusses with you how you taught the lesson, its good points, and things that you could have done to improve it.

Do not minimize the importance of formal observations and the conferences that follow them. Particularly if you are a new teacher, your observation reports will be a major factor in determining whether you are offered a contract for the following year. So prepare the best lesson that you can—the developmental lesson that was described earlier is often ideal in these situations. Begin with a question that leads to the aim of the lesson, and write the aim on the board. Ask questions of as many of your students as you can, questions which lead, in small steps, to an understanding of the aim. And as you proceed, note important concepts on the board. At the end of the lesson, review what students have learned, and refer back to the aim.

Evaluations

Evaluations are prepared at the end of the school year, and assess your overall performance. They are based on the observations that have been conducted during the year as well as other activities that you have been involved in, and usually include comments about your teaching performance and areas in which the evaluator feels you need to improve.

You will generally be invited to a conference in which the school administrator discusses your evaluation with you, and you will be asked to sign the formal evaluation report. In most cases, if you are unhappy with something in the evaluation report you will have the opportunity to write a statement to that effect.

If the tone of the evaluation conference and the evaluation report are negative, take that very seriously. Even if you are a seasoned teacher, negative evaluation reports are often precursors to disciplinary action or termination.

If your evaluation conference is generally negative and there is validity to the administrator's comments, ask for specific suggestions as to how you can improve. Thank the evaluator for his suggestions, and indicate that you will do everything that you can to improve in the coming year. If you feel that the evaluator's comments are not valid, try to discuss them with the evaluator, very tactfully. If that does not help, as soon as the conference is over, make an appointment to discuss the matter with your teachers' union or teachers' association representative.

PAPERWORK

When I was a college administrator, one of my responsibilities was to co-ordinate training programs that the college provided for businesses. I discussed training needs with our business clients, arranged for classes, and hired instructors to teach those classes. For some of the classes I hired regular faculty teaching what were called overload classes, extra classes for additional pay. And some of the instructors that I hired were part-time or adjunct staff.

One instructor I hired was very good in the classroom, and was also very popular with his students. But he had a reputation for being less than concerned about paperwork. He rarely turned in his class rosters or grades on time. I would call to remind him that they were due, and he would assure me that he would turn them in the very next day. And when they didn't arrive as he had promised, I would call him again. It took at least several calls before he turned in his class materials, often as much as several weeks late.

"Lighten up," you say, "he's a good teacher, and he is very popular with his students." The problem was that I had to forward instructors' class materials to the Registrar, and the Registrar was really unhappy with me when he didn't receive these materials promptly. Now, I could have told the Registrar that the instructor hadn't turned his materials in yet. But if I had, he would have told me, "You're in charge, get him to do it." In other words, when an instructor or teacher doesn't do what he is supposed to do, oftentimes the administrator "takes the heat."

But remember, this instructor was a really good teacher, and he was very popular among his students. What to do? The answer, after I finally received his materials—I determined that I would never again hire him to teach a class for me.

You see, every administrator reports to someone. In an elementary or secondary school, the assistant principal reports to the principal. The principal, perhaps, to the assistant superintendent. And the assistant superintendent reports to the superintendent. But even the superintendent is not without overseers. Remember, the superintendent reports to the school board.

The point is that many of the things that your administrator requires you to do may seem peripheral to your role as a teacher—even unimportant. But more often than not, your administrator's administrator requires them. And as often as not, it is that administrator's administrator who is "calling the shots." Understand this, and when your administrator requires that you do something that seems less important than your teaching, avoid problems for yourself by doing it as quickly and as efficiently as you can.

10

PLAYING BY THE RULES

In theory, there is no difference between theory and practice; in practice, there is.

SCHOOL DISTRICT PHILOSOPHY

Almost every school district has a formal, written, school district philosophy. Most school districts also have other similar documents such as a mission statement and a code of ethics. You should request copies of all these documents, and read them carefully.

Most of these documents are more general than specific, and are often written in somewhat abstract language. However, they are official documents, and represent how the school district feels it can best meet the needs of its young people. As an employee of the school district you are bound to accept and follow their dictates in these regards.

That is not to say that you are expected to be an automaton, acting without thinking, or that there is no opportunity for creativity in your teaching. Because of the general nature of these documents you almost always have a great deal of latitude, permitting widely different teaching styles and educational activities. But it is good to keep in mind that you are an employee of an organization, and that you have been hired to carry out their mandate in the general way that they have proscribed.

We're not talking about illegal or unethical behavior here. I've never personally seen an official school district document requiring staff members to do something that was illegal or unethical. But if you were to find yourself confronted with such a document, you should indicate to your immediate superior why you feel that the policy is objectionable. However, you should be aware of the fact that if you feel really strongly about your objections, it may become necessary for you to consider looking for employment elsewhere.

SCHOOL DISTRICT POLICY

School district policy is much more specific than school district philosophy, and in some cases, may be more difficult to obtain and keep track of. Actually, a better term would be school district policies, since it refers to a considerable number of distinct policies that have been established over a long period of time.

Keep in mind the fact that school district policies are not created at one time, as is the school district philosophy, but have been created over a long period of time. In fact, a school board may vote on a new item of policy at any school board meeting, and that policy then becomes part of the larger body of school district policies. And it is not at all uncommon, after a school board election, for a new school board to establish one or more policies that are diametrically opposed to previous policies. So school district policy is dynamic, constantly changing over time.

In many school districts, school district policies are kept in one place, and are fairly easily accessible. Unfortunately, some school districts are less well organized in this regard, and obtaining a copy of the district policy may be more difficult. In any event, it is a good idea to request a copy of the school district policy and to read whatever documents you receive, understanding, of course, that new policies can supercede old ones at any time.

SCHOOL BOARD MEMBERS

You are teaching a lesson, and a school board member comes into your classroom unannounced. He observes your lesson, and at the end of the class tells you that he did not like way you presented some part of the lesson. Or you are a school counselor, and a school board member asks you to change his son's English teacher. The school has a policy prohibiting the changing of students' teachers, but the school board member is insistent.

Do school board members have the authority to become involved in the daily operation of the school in these ways? School board members are elected officials, whose principal roles are to:

- establish school district policy,
- hire a chief school district administrator (often called a superintendent or district principal) to carry out that policy and manage the day-to-day operation of the schools in the district, and
- vote to approve or disapprove major expenditures, the hiring of new staff, and similar matters.

School board members carry out these roles by meeting regularly, and voting on issues as they arise.

It is important to understand that a school board member has no authority, except as a voting member of the school board. That is, a school board cannot come into a school and direct a member of the professional or support staff to perform some activity or to act, or not act, in a specific way. That is, at least, the theory. But we live in a world in which the line between theory and practice is sometimes blurred. Some school board members exceed their authority by directing staff members to perform particular activities. And since school administrators function in a political atmosphere, many administrators will not object when this occurs.

What do you do if a school board member exceeds his authority by asking you to carry out your duties in a specific way? I think, on a practical level, you have a few options:

- Do what the school board member requests without questioning him.

This is obviously the easiest route to take, and on a practical level if you feel insecure about objecting, just do what the school board member has requested. However, to protect yourself, I would suggest that as soon as possible after the event you make your immediate supervisor aware what has happened.

- Explain to the school board member, very tactfully, why you have acted as you did,

    If the school board member is reasonable, this is a viable option. But if he is not, be prepared for what may turn out to be an unpleasant encounter.

- Request support from your supervisor or administrator.

    If the school board member is insistent that you follow his directive, do as you are told, and discuss the matter with your immediate supervisor at the earliest possible time. It is generally unwise to tell a school board member that he has no authority to order you to do anything. He already knows that, and confrontation will most likely not serve your best interests. As always, tact and diplomacy are the keywords here.

CONFIDENTIALITY

A student tells you that he is using drugs. Or another, that she is pregnant. What are your rights, and your responsibilities?

Doctors, lawyers, religious leaders, and practitioners in a few other professions have what is called "privileged communication," which is popularly referred to as "confidentiality." Within certain limits, not only can they not repeat something that they have been told in confidence, but they are generally forbidden by law from doing so. Even in these cases, there are exceptions. If a person reveals that he is likely to hurt himself or someone else, privileged communication ceases to exist. In these cases, practitioners are duty bound to report what they have been told.

Generally, teachers, and even school counselors and school administrators, do not have privileged communication. Furthermore, many school districts have specific policies governing what kinds of information must be reported to administrators and parents. Find out if your school district has a written policy in this regard, and if it does, follow it to the letter. Failure to do so can subject you to dismissal, and in a legal action, can subject both you and your school to civil penalties.

This can create a real dilemma for teachers. You want students to talk to you, but if they tell you certain kinds of things, you must report what they have told you. If a student knows that you will report what he has told you, he may seek help or advice from a less reliable source. Or, he may not seek help or advice at all. While this may certainly be the case, you must remember that you work within a legal framework, and that you must act according to the dictates of that framework.

In some cases, you may want to be certain that students understand your responsibility before they tell you something that they want to remain confidential. As a high school counselor, I occasionally told students that if they told me certain kinds of things I was bound to report them to my administrator. After that admonition, sometimes, they told me what they had come to talk about, and sometimes they didn't.

Of course, it is important to understand that when a student tells you something of this sort, he is usually seeking help. Consequently, it is often possible to counsel the student to tell his parents what he has told you. On more than a few occasions, I have agreed to be present to lend moral support when a student told his parents what he had previously told me.

On one occasion, a young lady told me that voices were telling her to hurt herself. I arranged for the school psychologist to talk to her while I notified the school principal and called her parents. Her mother arrived shortly, and took her to a nearby hospital.

The young lady was hospitalized for about a year. After she was able to return to school, she would not speak to me. Whenever we passed one another in the hallway, she would look the other way. But I knew, of course, that I had done the right thing—actually, the only thing that I could have done under the circumstances. Sometimes, doing the right thing isn't the popular thing—and sometimes it isn't easy.

Interestingly, this young woman telephoned me about fifteen years later. She was living in another city, was married, and had a young child. She said, "I just wanted you to know that all those years ago you did the right thing."

It was nice to hear from her, and we chatted a little. I was happy to hear that she was doing well, and also that she realized that my revealing what she had told me was the right thing to do. But I know full well that people in these kinds of situations rarely come to that realization.

Always remember that there are times when doing the right thing isn't the popular thing. But still, you do it because it is the right thing to do.

WHAT'S A FERPA?—PART I

Are parents entitled to see their children's school records? The answer is usually an unqualified, "Yes." But there are some exceptions.

First, let's look at the case of most of the students you are likely to come into contact with—students who are under 18 years of age.

The Family Education Rights and Privacy Act (FERPA) is a federal law that was enacted in 1974 to protect the privacy of a student's educational records. It applies to all schools that receive federal funds from U.S. Department of Education programs—which includes almost all schools.

FERPA requires that schools provide parents with the right to inspect and review all of their children's educational records. Schools are not required to provide copies of these records except for reasons such as distance (although most schools will accede to a request for printed copies), and in those cases if copies are requested, schools may charge a fee for the copies.

Parents have the right to request that a school corrects records that they believe to be inaccurate or misleading. If the school does not comply with this request, parents may request a formal hearing. If, after that hearing the school decides not to change the records, parents have the right to place a statement in their child's records indicating their objections.

Schools must obtain written permission from a parent to release information about a student except to the following parties:

- school employees who have a need to know,
- schools to which the student is transferring,
- certain government officials in order to carry out lawful functions,
- appropriate parties in connection with financial aid to a student,

- organizations conducting certain studies for the school,
- accrediting organizations,
- individuals who have obtained court orders or subpoenas,
- persons who need to know in cases of health and safety emergencies, and
- state and local authorities, within a juvenile justice system, pursuant to state law.

Schools may disclose, without consent, directory information such as students' names, addresses, telephone numbers, dates and places of birth, honors and awards, and dates of attendance. However, schools that plan to release directory information must notify parents of that fact, and must give parents a reasonable amount of time to request that directory information about their children not be disclosed.

A later amendment to FERPA allows schools to withhold a document that a staff member has written about a student for which the student has signed a waiver of his right of access. This is often requested, although not required, in conjunction with student recommendations to colleges and universities. However, as a practical matter it is wise to assume that a student's parents, or the student himself, may someday have access to anything that you have written about him.

I have personally witnessed a number of instances in which private organizations and even public agencies have requested information to which they were not entitled. Do not accede to any request that you believe is in conflict with the provisions of FERPA. If this type of request is made to you, simply refer the person making the request to your school administrator.

WHAT'S A FERPA?—PART 2

FERPA applies to parents of students who are under 18 years of age. But it also gives those same rights to students who are:

- eighteen years of age or over, or
- under eighteen years of age, but attending a postsecondary school.

Furthermore, in the case of students in these two categories FERPA prohibits schools from releasing most kinds of information to the students' parents.

Does that mean that in the case of an eighteen-year-old student (or a student of any age who is attending a postsecondary institution), schools are prohibited from releasing information about the student's grades, and even his attendance, to the student's parent? You may be surprised, but the answer is an unqualified, "Yes."

There are a few exceptions that are required under an amendment to the Family Educational Right to Privacy Act. These generally involve information regarding the violation of a law, or the use or possession of controlled substances if the student is under the age of twenty-one.

If you are ever the least bit uncertain about whether to release information to the parent of a student in either of the above categories, do not hesitate to refer the parent to your administrator.

11

IT'S ALL ABOUT STUDENTS

The old believe everything,
the middle-aged suspect everything,
the young know everything.

Oscar Wilde

WHAT YOU SEE AND WHAT YOU DON'T

A new school administrator came to me one day, upset at something that had occurred as she walked past the school cafeteria. Two students were in a passionate embrace on the side of the cafeteria. As she passed, the administrator said, "This isn't the place for that."

The young man replied, "Where would you suggest we do it?"

I suggested that, "This isn't the place for that," was probably inviting trouble. Much better to say something like, "Stop that." The question then is, do you say, "Stop that," and wait to see that it has stopped? Or do you say it, and just keep walking?

I told her that we all choose what we see and what we don't. But once you choose to see something, it is usually difficult not to see it through to its conclusion. As a teacher you will often see things that shouldn't be going on. And it will be important for you to become good at quickly sizing up these situations:

- those that are really minor, and may best be ignored,
- those that are more serious, and need to be dealt with, and
- those that are serious, but that you feel insecure about your ability to deal with.

Those situations that are really minor,
and may best be ignored.

I am not suggesting that all minor infractions should be ignored. But all young people do things that they shouldn't from time to time. Sometimes you will want to intervene, and at other times you will want them to know that you've seen them without intervening (a sideways glance with raised eyebrows can be very effective). And sometimes, you will just prefer to ignore the situation.

Those situations that are more serious,
and need to be dealt with.

Police officers are taught to defuse situations and negotiate whenever possible. And unlike teachers, police officers carry weapons. As a teacher, your position is much more tenuous. Remember that negotiation is almost always preferable to confrontation. Be as firm as you feel you need to be, but not overly so. And try very hard not to become emotionally invested in the situation. Getting upset certainly won't help the situation—and it is sure to make you unhappy.

Those situations that are serious, but that you
feel insecure about your ability to deal with.

It should be obvious that it is foolhardy to become involved in a situation that you cannot see through to a successful conclusion. In these situations it is often best to just keep walking, actually, to walk a little more quickly, and to report the situation to an administrator or security guard immediately. The only thing you want to be certain that you do not do in a serious situation is ignore it.

BECOMING FRIENDLY WITH YOUR STUDENTS

Some teachers, particularly in the secondary grades, become friends of some of their students, going so far as to meet them socially after school and on weekends. Is that a good idea?

I think it is important to understand that there is a significant difference between being friendly to your students, and becoming their friend. I think the former is fine. While I know that there are teachers who will disagree, I'm not so sure that the latter is a particularly good idea.

First, I'm not sure that being a friend to your students makes educational sense. Actually, I think that being a friend to your students can sometimes get in the way of being an effective teacher. I once heard a group of students discussing something wrong that they had done. They knew that their teacher, whom they considered to be their friend, would find out about it. And they knew that when he did, he would have to report them to the school administration. So they decided to tell him what they had done before he found out. That way, they felt, he wouldn't feel comfortable about turning them in.

Another issue is one of fairness. If you are a friend to some of your students, do you think that it is possible to be completely fair to your other students? And even if it is, do you think that there will be the appearance of fairness to your other students? It is far better, I think, to be friendly to your students rather than to be their friend.

SEXUAL HARASSMENT

Title VII of The Civil Rights Act of 1964 deals with sexual harassment. Since the passage of The Civil Rights Act, the establishment of guidelines by the United States Equal Employment Opportunity Commission (EEOC) regarding what constitutes sexual harassment, and a number of highly publicized cases, sexual harassment is unquestionably on the decline. However, sexual harassment is far from completely eliminated in schools or in the workplace. That being the case, it is important that you know what sexual harassment is, and how to deal with any violations that you might encounter.

EEOC guidelines define two types of sexual harassment:

- quid pro quo sexual harassment, and
- hostile environment sexual harassment.

Quid Pro Quo Sexual Harassment

Quid pro quo means "this for that." In the case of sexual harassment, it refers to unwelcome sexual advances, requests for sexual favors, or other verbal or physical conduct with the understanding that submission to such conduct is either a term of an individual's employment or will be used as the basis for making decisions that affect the individual.

Hostile Environment Sexual Harassment

Hostile environment sexual harassment consists of unwelcome sexual advances, requests for sexual favors, and other verbal or physical conduct of a sexual nature when such conduct has the purpose or effect of unreasonably interfering with an individual's work performance, or creates an intimidating, hostile, or offensive working environment.

Both kinds of sexual harassment have occurred in schools. Although it is rare, there are occasional cases of quid pro quo sexual harassment in which a teacher asks a student for sexual favors in return for a better grade or other inducements, or in which an administrator asks a subordinate staff member for sexual favors in return for some work-related incentives.

More common, although also relatively rare, is hostile environment sexual harassment. A male teacher may make disparaging remarks about a female student, or female students in general, or a coworker may use sexually explicit language, for example, in the faculty lounge.

Understand that the person who feels harassed does not necessarily have to be a party to a conversation that is taking place. For example, a faculty member may be carrying on a sexually explicit conversation with someone over the telephone. Another faculty member within earshot of the conversation may claim sexual harassment, and the claim is very likely to be upheld.

Should you encounter any instances of sexual harassment, against a student, a staff member, or yourself, you should report it to the school administrator immediately. This is particularly important in the case of sexual harassment involving students, since they are likely to be more vulnerable and less well able to deal with these kinds of situations than are adults.

ACCEPTING GIFTS

In some schools it is not uncommon for students to give teachers gifts, particularly at holiday times. I have never felt comfortable about this practice—poorer children are likely to feel uneasy if their families cannot afford gifts for their teachers, and also, there is always the possibility that someone will wonder whether a teacher who received a gift from a student was more favorably disposed toward that student.

Both of these issues can be avoided by suggesting to students and parents, early in the school year, that while you sincerely appreciate the thought you feel uncomfortable about accepting gifts of any kind, and if proffered, you will return them.

On one occasion, when I was a high school teacher, a student's family had just returned from a trip to Las Vegas. Shortly after their return, the student offered me a money clip with an expensive chip from one of the Las Vegas casinos. I rejected the gift, thanking him, but telling him that I did not think that it would be appropriate for me to accept it. He told me, a few days later, that he had given the gift to another of his teachers.

Then, the following year the student asked me if I would change the grade I had assigned him the previous year. Five points more would have made him the school valedictorian. I told him, "No." But I could not help wondering if he had made a similar request of the teacher who had accepted the gift, and if he had, if that teacher had acceded to his request.

I was really happy not to have been in that situation myself.

STUDENT DRESS

When I first started teaching, school dress codes were common. In many schools, students could not wear jeans, and female students could not wear slacks of any kind. Many schools also had rules governing hair length.

All that changed in 1969 when the United States Supreme Court ruled in Tinker v. Des Moines Independent Community School District (393 U.S. 503, 89 S, Ct. 733 (1969)) that school officials' rights in this area are constrained by the federal Constitution. More specifically, students have the right of expression in school, and this right extends to student dress, unless ". . . the exercise of that right would materially and substantially interfere with the requirements of appropriate discipline or collide with the rights of others in the school."

The Supreme Court decision was not unanimous, and was not without dissent. And it should be added that when cases involving, for example, student hair length have been heard in the courts, different decisions have been handed down by different federal circuit courts. That said, the Supreme Court decision became, and remains, the law of the land.

Of course, it can be argued that a big hairdo, a very skimpy outfit, or a shirt with certain words printed on it interfere with learning—and consequently, with the rights of others in the school. But schools' authority in this area was certainly limited by this Supreme Court decision.

The situation has become more complex over time as the political climate in the country has become more conservative. In fact, in many places communities are now instituting student dress codes and occasionally even uniforms, sometimes to prevent the wearing of gang "colors," and sometimes because the communities feel that students who are dressed more formally perform better academically.

There have been relatively few court cases concerning student dress, but there have been a significant number of cases involving hair length. The United States Supreme Court declined to hear these cases until 1976, when it agreed to hear a case involving grooming regulations of the Suffolk County New York Police Department (Kelley v. Johnson, 425 U.S. 238 (1976)).

The Suffolk County Police Department prohibited officers from wearing long or bushy hear, long sideburns, mustaches, or beards. After hearing the case, the Supreme Court ruled that the burden was on the police department to demonstrate a "public need" for the regulation.

While this decision would seem, by extension, to have resolved the matter as it concerns students, there are some differences. For example, while an employee has the right to leave a job, in most cases students cannot leave school. When the issue involving students' hair length has been litigated, there have been differing decisions in various circuit courts.

And, the issue of student uniforms which have been adopted by some schools has not yet been tested in the courts.

So while there are broad legal guidelines in the matter of student dress and grooming, in this regard, the jury is still out.

CORPORAL PUNISHMENT

Early in my teaching career I was shocked to see student records with the notation, "paddle one," "paddle two," and "paddle three." Not only were students being routinely paddled in the school district's junior high school, but the punishment was being noted in their school records.

Today, corporal punishment is prohibited in every industrialized country in the world except the United States, Canada, and one state in Australia. In the United States more than half the states, 27 in all, currently prohibit corporal punishment. In the other states, corporal punishment is permitted in some school districts, and prohibited in others.

Whether permitted or not, there are a number of reasons why corporal punishment is a bad idea. And if you work in a state and a school in which it is permitted, they are equally good reasons for you not to employ it.

- Studies have shown that while corporal punishment will stop a child from misbehaving, the child's compliance usually lasts for only a short time. That is, the child most often misbehaves again in a relatively short time.
- In some cases, corporal punishment leads to child abuse. While this is generally more true of corporal punishment in the home, it has also occurred in some instances in which corporal punishment has been employed in schools.

- Corporal punishment can cause unintended but very serious physical injury.
- It trains a child to use violence, both as a child and into his adulthood.

WRITING RECOMMENDATIONS

If you work in a high school, it is very likely that students will at least occasionally ask you to write college or job recommendations for them. Before getting into the mechanics of the process, remember that according to the Family Education Rights and Privacy Act (FERPA), the parents of students under the age of 18, and students over the age of 18 or who are enrolled in a post secondary institution, have the right to access all their records at a school.

While some schools ask students to sign a waiver regarding teacher recommendations, you should assume that students may eventually see anything that you write about them. This, of course, will never be a problem if you never write anything detrimental about a student. As a matter of fact, for this reason as well as a number of others, I believe that if you do not feel that you can write a positive recommendation for a student, it is probably best to decline the student's request and not to write any recommendation for him.

There are two problems that you are likely to encounter when students ask you to write recommendations for them. First, writing recommendations can be very time consuming. To further complicate matters, you may not know enough about a student to feel comfortable about writing a helpful recommendation.

One way of dealing with both of these problems is to ask students to write an outline of the recommendation that they would like you to write for them. Ask students to include the following information in their outlines:

- academics, including best subjects, honors and special classes that they have taken, and special projects,
- extra curricular activities and offices held,
- sports,

- community activities,
- hobbies and other interests,
- honors and awards, and
- anything else that will make the student look good.

Of course, you don't have to include everything that the student includes in his outline in your recommendation. But once you have a student's outline, writing a recommendation for him should be relatively easy.

DIVORCE

These days, many children grow up in one-parent homes. Since these children frequently bring special problems to their school experience, they require special understanding and support.

A number of studies have undertaken to investigate the differences between children of divorced families, and those from "intact" families. Most of the studies have shown that children from divorced families are, on average, somewhat more likely to experience problems than children from intact families. That is certainly not to say that all children from divorced families experience problems in or out of school. But the evidence strongly suggests that they are more likely to experience such problems.

These problems are often the result of a number of factors:

- **Economic Loss.** Children of divorced families generally have more limited economic resources.
- **Parental Loss.** Because children of divorced families have less contact with one parent, they often have less emotional support.
- **Increased Life Stress.** Divorced children often undergo more changes in their home lives, which often creates additional stress for them.
- **Parental Stress.** Parents involved in divorce are frequently more stressed than other parents, and this stress often impacts on their children.
- **Exposure to Parental Conflict.** If there is conflict between a child's parents, the child is likely to be affected by it.

- **Guilt.** Children of divorced families frequently feel guilty because of feelings that in some way they may have been responsible for the divorce.

As a teacher, you cannot solve any of these problems. But you can be sensitive to them, and also to the fact that these children may be particularly fragile, or may even act out as a result of things that are going on in their home lives.

A related issue that you may find yourself confronted with is the situation in which a non-custodial parent requests information about a child. Unless there are court documents that prevent the non-custodial parent from having contact with or obtaining information about the child, the parent is entitled to that information. However, it is often best to notify the appropriate school administrator of the request before you comply with it.

ADD AND ADHD

Tim is a very friendly six-year-old. But he is having trouble learning to read, and he can't seem to sit still for more than a few minutes. Not too many years ago, he would have been labeled "hyperactive." In fact, Tim's mother says that he is hyperactive. But you wonder if it isn't Attention Deficit Disorder (ADD).

If he does suffer from ADD, Tim is far from alone. Four to six percent of the population, both children and adults, is considered to have some form of attention deficit disorder. As a teacher, you are likely to encounter a considerable number of ADD students in the course of your teaching career. In fact, it is not uncommon to encounter more than one ADD student in just one class. The primary symptoms of ADD are:

- poor attention span—distractibility, and
- weak impulse control.

In addition to these two symptoms, some students also exhibit a third symptom:

- hyperactivity.

Poor Attention Span—Distractibility

The student is unable to maintain attention to tasks. You direct your class to read a passage, for example, and within a few minutes, perhaps even sooner, you notice that one of your students is looking out the window. Of course, this could happen to any student, but it is a consistent pattern for this student.

Weak Impulse Control

You find that you are constantly reminding the student not to call out in class, but he continues to do so. He isn't a bad boy. But he just can't seem to control himself.

Hyperactivity

Not all ADD students are hyperactive, but those who are are excessively active and restless. No matter how many times you remind them to remain in their seats, they are constantly up and around the room. They just cannot seem to sit still in their seats. When hyperactivity is present, the condition is usually referred to as Attention Deficit Hyperactivity Disorder—ADHD.

The majority of ADD and ADHD students are boys, but many girls are also affected. When they have the condition, however, girls are less likely to be hyperactive. That is, girls are more likely to be ADD than ADHD.

ADD and ADHD are by no means new conditions. They were recognized as long ago as the beginning of the twentieth century—in 1902, to be exact. But it was not until more recently that these conditions have been recognized as having a biological basis. ADD and ADHD show up in brain scans and in genetic studies, and they are responsive to medication.

If you have one or more ADD students in your class, you should discuss the problem with the school psychologist and the school counselor, and also with the child's parents. ADD and ADHD may be regarded as handicapping conditions, and the child may be eligible for special services.

There is considerable controversy about medicating children with ADD and ADHD. Ritalin and similar drugs have been used very successfully with many of these youngsters. However, these central nervous system stimulants are very potent drugs, and are not without significant side effects (most notably, insomnia and weight loss).

Another approach, although controversial, that seems to work with some ADD and ADHD children is a diet that eliminates certain foods from the child's diet. This diet was developed by Dr. Benjamin Feingold, a pediatrician and professor of pediatric medicine, and consequently, is referred to as the Feingold Diet.

While keeping a child on a diet is certainly more difficult than administering a pill a few times each day, some parents prefer it to chemical intervention. For parents who would like see if the Feingold diet benefits their children, the Feingold Association provides considerable information about the diet, and also provides emotional support for the families of ADD and ADHD children. Their web site, located at www.feingold.org, provides a wealth of information about ADD and ADHD, and about the Feingold Diet.

But what can you, as a teacher, do to help an ADD or ADHD student?

1. You can communicate your observations and concerns with the school psychologist and counselor. In addition to being able to document your observations, these colleagues may be able to suggest ways in which you can help the student. They may also be able to obtain additional services for the student, and to provide additional support for him.
2. You can discuss your observations with the student's parents. Understand that the parents are most likely frustrated with the problems that their child is experiencing, and will likely be very appreciative for your suggestions and assistance.
3. And, you can be particularly sensitive to the student's needs, understanding that when he is difficult to manage it is not because he wants to be difficult, but because his behavior is beyond his control.

Some ADD students outgrow their condition, but some remain ADD all their lives. Some of those who do not outgrow the condition will be affected throughout their lives. But fortunately, in most cases they will learn to compensate for it, and will be able to lead useful and productive lives.

STUDENTS WHO ARE TOO ENTHUSIASTIC . . . AND STUDENTS WHO ARE NOT ENTHUSIASTIC ENOUGH

Almost every class has a student who is just too enthusiastic. He wants to answer every question—in fact, his hand usually goes up even before you finish asking a question. On the other hand, and equally frustrating, are the students who never volunteer to answer any questions. Really effective teachers know how to handle both types of students in ways that improve the educational experience for them, and for all the students in their classes.

Students Who Are Too Enthusiastic

Students who are always volunteering to answer questions are probably the more frustrating of the two. While it is certainly flattering to have students who are extremely interested in what you are teaching and extremely eager to please you, the novelty usually wears thin pretty quickly. It's not unlike eating too much ice cream—well, perhaps that's a bad analogy.

The problem, of course, is that these students crave your attention and approval. They are often insecure, and in some instances, may not get very much attention and approval at home. You can't have them dominating class discussions, but on the other hand you don't want to make them feel even more insecure than they already are.

The solution is to give these students the attention and approval that they need, but to keep them from dominating your class discussions. There are a few things that you can do to achieve this:

1. Speak to these students privately. Tell them that you know that they usually know the right answer, and that you are proud of them for that, but that you have to call on other students too.

2. Praise them in class for knowing so many answers without calling on them. "I know you know the right answer, John, but I would like Mary to answer this time."

3. Give these students extra responsibilities in your class. Have them take messages to the office, accompany students to the nurse, and help students who need extra help. And praise them each time they do one of these things for being so helpful.

Remember, your goal is to give these students the attention and approval that they need, but to channel their enthusiasm into activities and behaviors that keep them from monopolizing your class discussions.

Students Who Are Not Enthusiastic Enough

At the other end of the spectrum are the students who are not enthusiastic enough—who never volunteer to answer a question. It could be that these students don't know the answers to your questions. But more commonly, they are insecure or embarrassed. They are usually afraid that they will answer a question incorrectly.

Understanding that these students' reluctance to become involved is usually the result of embarrassment or fear should give you considerable insight into how to deal with them.

1. For those students who don't volunteer to answer questions because they are less capable than their classmates, periodically ask a few questions that even your weakest students are capable of answering. Give them the opportunity to succeed, and praise them when they do.

2. Whenever you ask a question, wait a few seconds before calling on a student to answer. This gives all your students a chance to try to answer it.

3. Don't only call on students who volunteer. Call on some students who don't volunteer, to encourage all your students to try to answer your questions.

4. Be certain that students do not feel embarrassed for having answered a question incorrectly. When a student answers a question incorrectly, say something like, "That's not what I'm looking for,

but I can see that you've given the question some really serious thought," or, ". . . I like the way you're thinking," or, ". . . you're really on the right track."

Your goal, of course, is to get all your students to participate in classroom discussions, but to prevent some students from dominating them. With a little practice, you should be able to achieve both of these goals.

NEVER DISCOURAGE A STUDENT . . . ANY STUDENT

Winston Churchill was a stutterer. As a child, one of his teachers warned his mother, "Because of his stuttering he should be discouraged from following in his father's political footsteps."

And then there was the friend of mine whose mother met one of his former high school teachers while she was shopping. My friend hadn't been an exemplary student in high school, and the teacher asked his mother if he had managed to graduate from college. His mother told the teacher that he had graduated from medical school, and was just completing his residency.

There are thousands of similar stories. In fact, something similar may have happened to you. Most certainly, it has happened to someone you know. Always keep in mind that when you tell someone that they will succeed, they usually will. But when you tell them that they will not succeed, they almost invariably won't. It couldn't be simpler.

I once worked in a high school in which we had H (honors) classes, R (regular) classes, and X (modified) classes. The less able students were, "X students!" We, their teachers, knew what that meant. But, of course, our students also knew what that meant.

And then there was the young hairdresser who was cutting my hair. When I mentioned that I was a teacher, she told me, "I'm not very smart. I was one of the dumb kids in school." Imagine, not only did she think that she was not smart when she was in school, but she saw herself as having been "dumb." And while she was quite successful in the line of work that she had chosen—at age 27 she owned the salon—she still saw herself as "dumb." How incredibly sad. Of course, I told her that she didn't seem "dumb" to me. But I doubt that after having heard the opposite as many times as she had, my comments had much impact.

The well-known writer and teacher Neil Postman once said, "If we're going to categorize students as 'gifted,' 'honors,' 'regular,' and 'modified' students, we ought to categorize teachers into those categories as well." Of course, teachers would never allow themselves to be categorized in those ways. But we do it with students all the time.

But what if your school classifies students into classes based on "ability levels." What can you as a teacher do? Understand that I am not suggesting that heterogeneous classes are better than homogeneous classes. I suspect that they are not, but there is considerable controversy and debate surrounding that issue. Whatever the answer, there are things that teachers can do to minimize any ill effects that may be caused by ability grouping.

Very specifically, I am suggesting that as teachers we do everything in our power to tell our students, all our students, that they are important, and that they have the ability to be successful. No, not just that they have the ability to succeed, but that they WILL succeed. We need to do it all the time—every day, and in every class. And we need to do it the most with our least capable students, because they are the students who need it the most.

An option for high schools that group students according to ability levels is to eliminate the traditional designations and allow students to self-select their classes. If the class titles are appropriately descriptive, students will select classes for themselves that are appropriate without the designations. I expect that very few less able students will elect to take, "Existential Philosophy in Twentieth Century Literature," when "Popular Sports Stories" is another option. Perhaps, some day you can suggest it at your school. Or perhaps, some day as a school administrator you will be instrumental in getting your school to adopt such a system.

WHAT TEACHING IS REALLY ABOUT

Whitwell, Tennessee is a small town of only 1,600, not far from where teacher John T. Scopes was tried and convicted of teaching Darwin's

Theory of Evolution in 1925. It is a white, Christian community—there are no Jews, no Catholics, no Asians, and only a small handful of Blacks and Hispanics.

In 1968, Whitwell Middle School's deputy principal attended a teacher-training course in Chattanooga, and decided to use the Holocaust as a tool for teaching tolerance. Not to mention the students, many of the townspeople knew little or nothing about the Holocaust. The course was offered after school hours, on a voluntary basis.

The students were awed by the sheer number of Jews who were killed by the Nazis. The number, 6,000,000, was incomprehensible to them. One girl suggested that the students collect 6,000,000 paperclips and turn them into a sculpture as a tribute to the victims. A club was formed, and a project was born.

The project attracted the attention of two German journalists, and after they wrote about the project, other writers became interested in it as well. As a result, paperclips began arriving from all over the world; from ordinary people, and even from some very famous people. Even President Clinton sent a letter and some paperclips. The club has become the most popular organization in Whitwell Middle School, with more students wanting to join than can be accommodated.

In addition to the paperclip project and an annual trip to the Holocaust Museum in Washington, the students participate in a number of other activities, all designed to further not only their understanding of the Holocaust, but also their tolerance for other people.

These students will carry what they have learned, not just about the Holocaust, but about tolerance, interpersonal relations, empathy, patience, and a host of other things for the rest of their lives. They will remember these things, and their lives will have been unalterably changed by them long after they have forgotten, for example, the Pythagorean theorem.

And isn't that, after all, what education is really all about.

12

FINDING A JOB

My grandfather once told me that there were two kinds of people:
those who do the work and those who take the credit. He told me to
try to be in the first group; there was much less competition.

Indira Gandhi

YOUR RESUME

If you have a job, you may be thinking, "Why do I need a resume?" If
you are reasonably sure that you are going to be at your current job "for
the duration," you may not need one. But even then, it is useful to have
an updated resume in your file or stored on your computer. Occasionally, as during a school's reaccreditation, your administrator may ask you
for an up-to-date resume. Or a resume may prove invaluable when the
perfect part-time job comes along some day when you least expect it. Of
course, if you don't currently have a job, or if you will be looking for a
new job, a resume will be invaluable.

Over the years, I have seen many, many resumes. I suppose you could
say that the resumes I have seen approximate a bell-shaped curve. Most
have been acceptable—average, actually, and unexciting. A few have

been terrible, and a very few have been really outstanding. Interestingly, preparing an outstanding resume takes very little more time and effort than preparing an average or poor one. Here's how you can prepare a really outstanding resume.

When most people prepare their resume, they think about themselves—they ask themselves, "What can I tell a prospective employer about myself?" It sounds logical, but is actually a less than ideal approach. Much better, I think, is to begin by thinking about your prospective employer. Ask yourself, "What is important to him or her?" And also ask yourself, "What is he or she looking for?" With that in mind, let's go through the process of creating a resume.

Of course, you will begin your resume with some identifying information: your name, address, telephone number, and if you have one, your e-mail address. And you will also indicate the position that you are looking for.

The next item that I am going to suggest that you include in your resume is one that is missing from at least ninety-five percent of the resumes that I have seen, and probably ninety-five percent of all resumes—a statement indicating what you can do for a prospective employer. That's right. I'm suggesting that you want to tell prospective employers, right after your name and address and the position that you are looking for, what you can do for them in very specific terms.

But before you write your statement, let's explore what kind of employees a prospective employer is looking for. Start by making a list of the things that you think a school administrator is looking for when he staffs his school. After you create your list, take a look at mine. I think that most school administrators are looking for teachers who:

- know their subject matter,
- are able to teach effectively,
- care about their students,
- communicate well with students' parents,
- are conscientious,
- work hard,
- are creative,
- work well with their colleagues,
- take direction well from supervisors,

- act professionally, and
- complete their clerical responsibilities in a timely fashion.

Compare your list with mine. Revise yours if you would like to, and then write a statement that will appear in your resume under the heading, "What A Prospective Employer Can Expect." Don't make it too long, but don't hesitate to write three or four sentences if you need to.

Here's what one new teacher's resume looks like so far:

John Smith

123 First Street
New York, NY 10001
(212) 987-6543
Jsmith123@educate.com

Position Sought: English Teacher

What a Prospective Employer Can Expect

My employer can expect that I will perform all my teaching and related activities professionally and efficiently. I will work hard, be sensitive to the needs of my students, and will do my best to communicate effectively, when necessary, with their parents. I understand that I am a member of a team, and will work well with my colleagues, take direction from the school administration, complete administrative responsibilities promptly, and support the goals of the schools and school district.

Believe it or not, you have already completed the most important part of your resume. Now you can get on with the rest of your resume—the easy part. Many resumes include academic information next, the degrees and certifications that the applicant has. I would prefer to include what I consider to be more important information next—your experience.

Include your experience in chronological order, with the most recent item first. Indicate the position that you held, and the dates that you held it. You will want to explain your responsibilities, but be sure to indicate not only what your responsibilities were, but also how you carried out your responsibilities better or differently from the way the ordinary person would have carried them out. For example:

Windham Middle School
September, 2001–June, 2002
Student Teacher

I taught one tenth-grade English class every day, and various other classes on a rotating basis. In addition to the required coursework, my tenth-grade English class concentrated on reading improvement. At the end of the year, we achieved the greatest improvement in reading scores in the school on the statewide examinations.

Note that the applicant described where he worked, and when, and he also described his work responsibilities. But even more important, he indicated accomplishments which set him apart from the "average" job applicant.

Include any other experience that you may have had. If you are new to teaching, don't hesitate to include non-teaching employment or volunteer activities that you may have had. For each, indicate accomplishments, and any skills that you may have gained that have relevance for a teacher.

The rest is pretty straight forward. Include, in separate sections, the things you normally see in resumes: special skills that you may have, honors, awards and publications, and your academic credentials and certifications.

Some people will tell you that resumes should be only one page in length—that employers don't want to read more than one page. If you can get everything onto one page, that's fine. But if you need more than one page, and most people do, don't hesitate to use a second page. Just be sure to put the most important things on the first page. Most employers will read a subsequent page or even two subsequent pages, if they like what they see on the first page.

That's it. Your "super" resume hardly took you longer to prepare than an "ordinary" resume. But it looks much better, and will be much, much more helpful as you search for an appropriate job. Oh, don't forget to print your resume on paper that is a little better than standard paper. Paper that is slightly heavier than standard 24 lb. paper, with a slight off-white color, will make your resume stand out. Avoid darker color paper and shading, as resumes are frequently faxed from one office to another and those elements don't fax well.

FINDING A TEACHING JOB

In some places jobs are plentiful—you can apply for a teaching job today and start working tomorrow. But in other places jobs are few and far between. Obviously, it's a matter of supply and demand. In areas where there are many unfilled teaching positions but not enough qualified applicants to fill those positions, jobs are very easy to find. But where there are more qualified applicants than teaching positions, finding a teaching job can be extremely difficult.

If you are looking for a teaching job, try to assess the job situation in the geographic areas that you are interested in. You can often find this information in local newspapers, on the Internet, by calling school districts, and by contacting local teachers' associations or unions.

In some places where there is an oversupply of qualified candidates, only a small percentage of applicants may actually find jobs. You may find that you will have to substitute teach for a year or two before you find something. And even then, there is no guarantee that you will be offered a full-time job.

In those cases, if you are able to relocate to an area where teaching jobs are plentiful you may want to consider doing that. There are a number of areas in the United States in which there is an abundance of teaching jobs, generally because of rapidly growing populations in those areas. I have known young teachers who have been offered jobs in some of these areas after only a telephone interview.

When you look for a job, remember that in reality you are marketing yourself. You need to do whatever you can do to make yourself stand out from among all the other qualified applicants for that job.

One young teacher I know who was looking for a job in an area where the job market was very competitive developed an interesting marketing plan. He wrote a booklet that he called, "A Teacher's Guide to the Internet." It was designed to help teachers who are unfamiliar with the Internet learn how to use it, and then, described ways in which teachers can use the Internet with their classes.

After he wrote the booklet, he had copies made, and sent a copy, along with a cover letter and a copy of his resume, to the principals of all the schools in the area that he was interested in teaching in.

Now I'm certainly not suggesting that you write a booklet about the Internet and send it with a letter to school districts that you would like to work for—for one thing, it has already been done. But if you can think of some novel way to market yourself, some way that will make you stand out from all the other applicants in a tight job market, by all means do it.

INTERVIEWING FOR A JOB

Most job candidates see a job interview as a technique that an employer uses to determine whether he wants to hire a job candidate. But actually, a job interview is much more than that.

- Certainly, a job interview enables an employer to find out about you.

John Smith

123 First Street
New York, NY 10001
(212) 987-6543
Jsmith123@educate.com

Dear School Principal,

In just a few years, the Internet has become a significant part of American life. As you know, the Internet has important implications for both students and teachers. Unfortunately, not all teachers are familiar with the Internet, or how to use it in their classrooms.

To help these teachers, I have prepared a booklet, "A Teacher's Guide to the Internet." I have enclosed a copy of the booklet. While it is copyrighted, I am happy to give you permission to photocopy it and distribute it freely to any members of your staff that you think might find it useful.

Since I am looking for a job as a secondary school social studies teacher, I have also enclosed a copy of my resume. Of course, the booklet is yours to use even if you are not currently in the market for a hard-working, creative social studies teacher. But if you are, I would be very interested in talking to you about my qualifications, and how I might be able to help enhance your program.

Very truly yours,

(Signature)

- A job interview also enables you to find out about the job, and the employer.
- Perhaps most significantly, a job interview enables you to tell the interviewer about your qualifications—in other words, to sell yourself.

But before you report for any job interview, it is important that you do some homework. You want to know as much about the school and the school district as you possibly can in advance of your interview. Many school districts have web sites that provide information about the school district, its goals, and its population. You may also be able to obtain this kind of information from other sources on the Internet, such as local newspapers and state departments of education. And, you can almost always obtain a wealth of very useful information by telephoning the local teachers' association or teachers' union. Having information about the community and student body, and perhaps also about the principal, will be invaluable to you in presenting yourself in the most favorable light.

A Job Interview Enables an Employer to Find Out about You

An effective interviewer can learn a great deal about you, not only by what you say, but also by watching the way you conduct yourself.

Begin by dressing appropriately for an interview. For men this means slacks, a jacket and a tie, and for women, a skirt and blouse, dress, or suit. You may wonder if it is necessary to mention this, but it is surprising how many job seekers ignore what should be obvious. On one occasion, for example, I interviewed a young man for a teaching job who arrived wearing jeans and a polo shirt. He had good qualifications, but because he was inappropriately dressed for the interview, he was immediately dropped from consideration.

When you enter the room, extend your hand to the interviewer, and say, "Hello, I'm (your name). I'm pleased to meet you." Practice this a few times in front of a mirror before your interview so that you feel comfortable doing it. After you introduce yourself, wait for the interviewer to invite you to take a seat. Be sure to make eye contact during the interview, and remember to smile, and to answer questions directly. When the interview is over, thank the interviewer for meeting with you.

A Job Interview Enables You to Find Out about the Job

Use the interview to find out about the job. You will almost always be given an opportunity to ask questions—have several prepared beforehand. Your questions will not only help you to obtain information about the school and the school district, but will tell the interviewer more about you. So ask questions that indicate your professionalism:

- "What is the student population like?"
- "What is the school district's philosophy?"
- "How supportive is the community?"

Don't ask questions about sick leave and employee benefits. While these things are important, if you are offered a job you will receive detailed information about them before you are asked to sign a contract.

A Job Interview Enables You to Sell Yourself

Most significantly, a job interview enables you to sell yourself. Plan for your interview by making a list of things that you want to tell the interviewer about yourself. And try to work those things into the answers to the questions that you are asked.

For example, suppose that you really want to tell an interviewer about an innovative math program that you have introduced in your last school, but the interviewer asks you only for your ideas about teaching reading. You will certainly want to begin by answering the interviewer's question about reading. But then, after you have answered the question about reading you might say something like, "In addition to reading, I've been involved in a really exciting math program. Would you like to hear about it?"

The Post Interview Letter

And finally, write a short note to the interviewer as soon as possible after the interview thanking him for interviewing you and expressing your interest in the job. Everyone knows that they should do this, but it is surprising how few job seekers actually do it. Writing a follow-up letter to the interviewer cannot but promote your application.

Dear Mr. Smith,

Thank you very much for taking the time out of your very busy schedule to talk to me about working at Eastwood Middle School. I was very impressed with the school, its educational program, and the school district's mission.

If I can provide you with any additional information about myself, please do not hesitate to contact me.

Very truly yours,

(Signature)

13

SURVIVING YOUR FIRST YEAR . . .
AND BEYOND

Success is the ability to go from failure to failure without losing your
enthusiasm.

Winston Churchill

DEALING WITH THE SYSTEM

Every year I see some students, who are intelligent enough to be very
successful in college, dropping out. It happens in community colleges,
and it happens in four-year colleges and universities. It even happens,
although to a lesser degree, in schools that admit only students with very
impressive high school records.

There are a number of reasons why this is the case. But whatever the
reasons, I try to encourage my students to succeed, not just in my class,
but in all their classes. To this end, I begin each of my college classes
with the following "pep talk."

Success in college does not require a high level of intelligence. Certainly, in-
telligence makes it easier, but there are lots of highly intelligent people who
are less than successful in college. I'll bet you know at least a few of them.

So if it isn't intelligence, what does it take to be successful in college?
The answer should be fairly obvious. Success in college requires that
you understand the system, and that you do what the system requires.
A major part of that is discovering what your professors want. And once
you discover what they want, giving it to them.

"Not fair," you say. "It shouldn't be that way." My response is, "You
may be right, but that is the way that it is. And if you want to be suc-
cessful in college, you need to do it."

And not only is that the way it is in college, that's the way life is. To be
successful in your job, or in almost any other aspect of your life, you need
to understand the system, and then, to do what it requires.

You've already demonstrated that you know this. You've graduated
from college (or you have almost graduated), and you've become certified to teach school (or almost become certified). But now you have to
learn how another system works, the system in the school that has hired
you. You have to determine what the system wants, and you have to do
what the system wants.

But based on your background, it shouldn't be particularly difficult.
You have demonstrated that you have been able to graduate from college. Now all you have to do is adapt what you have done in college to
the next important stage of your life.

THINKING ABOUT RETIREMENT

I know, I know, you're only twenty-two years old. Retirement is so incredibly far off. But the fact is that you should start thinking about retirement today. Right now!

Consider the following scenario. Two college graduates begin teaching together. The first teacher invests $2,000 a year in an Individual Re-
tirement Account (IRA) the first year, and in each of the following six
years. The second invests nothing for the first six years, but then invests
$2,000 in each succeeding year until he retires at age sixty-two. Con-
sidering a very conservative 11 percent rate of return, here are the results.

Notice that Teacher 1 invested only $14,000, all during the first seven
years of his employment, but at age sixty-two he has accumulated

Retirement Calculator

Assumptions:
1. 11 percent appreciation per year.
2. Retirement at age 62.

Age	Teacher 1		Teacher 2		Teacher 3	
	Investment	Value	Investment	Value	Investment	Value
22	2,000.00	2,220.00	-		2,000.00	2,220.00
23	2,000.00	4,684.20	-		2,000.00	4,684.20
24	2,000.00	7,419.46	-		2,000.00	7,419.46
25	2,000.00	10,455.60	-		2,000.00	10,455.60
26	2,000.00	13,825.72	-		2,000.00	13,825.72
27	2,000.00	17,566.55	-		2,000.00	17,566.55
28	2,000.00	21,718.87	2,000.00	220.00	2,000.00	21,718.87
29	-	24,107.94	2,000.00	2,464.20	2,000.00	26,327.94
30	-	26,759.82	2,000.00	4,955.26	2,000.00	31,444.02
31	-	29,703.40	2,000.00	7,720.34	2,000.00	37,122.86
32	-	32,970.77	2,000.00	10,789.58	2,000.00	43,426.37
33	-	36,597.56	2,000.00	14,196.43	2,000.00	50,423.28
34	-	40,623.29	2,000.00	17,978.04	2,000.00	58,189.84
35	-	45,091.85	2,000.00	22,175.62	2,000.00	66,810.72
36	-	50,051.95	2,000.00	26,834.94	2,000.00	76,379.90
37	-	55,557.67	2,000.00	32,006.79	2,000.00	87,001.69
38	-	61,669.01	2,000.00	37,747.53	2,000.00	98,791.87
39	-	68,452.60	2,000.00	44,119.76	2,000.00	111,878.98
40	-	75,982.39	2,000.00	51,192.93	2,000.00	126,405.66
41	-	84,340.45	2,000.00	59,044.16	2,000.00	142,530.29
42	-	93,617.90	2,000.00	67,759.01	2,000.00	160,428.62
43	-	103,915.87	2,000.00	77,432.51	2,000.00	180,295.77
44	-	115,346.62	2,000.00	88,170.08	2,000.00	202,348.30
45	-	128,034.74	2,000.00	100,088.79	2,000.00	226,826.61
46	-	142,118.57	2,000.00	113,318.56	2,000.00	253,997.54
47	-	157,751.61	2,000.00	128,003.60	2,000.00	284,157.27
48	-	175,104.28	2,000.00	144,304.00	2,000.00	317,634.57
49	-	194,365.76	2,000.00	162,397.44	2,000.00	354,794.37
50	-	215,745.99	2,000.00	182,481.15	2,000.00	396,041.76
51	-	239,478.05	2,000.00	204,774.08	2,000.00	441,826.35
52	-	265,820.63	2,000.00	229,519.23	2,000.00	492,647.25
53	-	295,060.90	2,000.00	256,986.34	2,000.00	549,058.44
54	-	327,517.60	2,000.00	287,474.84	2,000.00	611,674.87
55	-	363,544.54	2,000.00	321,317.07	2,000.00	681,179.11
56	-	403,534.44	2,000.00	358,881.95	2,000.00	758,328.81
57	-	447,923.23	2,000.00	400,578.97	2,000.00	843,964.98
58	-	497,194.78	2,000.00	446,862.65	2,000.00	939,021.13
59	-	551,886.21	2,000.00	498,237.55	2,000.00	1,044,533.45
60	-	612,593.69	2,000.00	555,263.68	2,000.00	1,161,652.13
61	-	679,978.99	2,000.00	618,562.68	2,000.00	1,291,653.87
62	-	754,776.68	2,000.00	688,824.58	2,000.00	1,435,955.79

$754,776.68—more than three-quarters of a million dollars. Teacher 2, on the other hand, invested $2,000 a year for 35 years, a total of $70,000, yet when he retires, he has accumulated almost $66,000 less than Teacher 1.

I've also included data for Teacher 3, who invested $2,000 during each year that he was employed. As you can see, Teacher 3 has accumulated almost one-and-one-half million dollars.

Of course, no one can promise that your investment will return 11 percent per year. It may return more, or it may return less. But whatever the rate of return, the fact remains that the earlier you start saving for retirement, the more money you will have available when you do retire.

I know that it isn't easy to invest $2,000 each year, particularly in the early years when your salary is lower and you may have educational loans to repay. But remember that the early years affect your total savings much, much more than the later years. Start saving as soon as you start working and save whatever you can, even if it is only a small amount from each paycheck.

CONSERVING YOUR ENERGY

I was fortunate in having the opportunity to study with, and get to know, Dr. Neil Postman while I was a graduate student at New York University. I was particularly interested in a textbook that Dr. Postman had written, *Discovering Your Language*, (Neil Postman, Harold Morine [and] Greta Morine, [New York]: Holt, Rinehart and Winston, 1963), which used linguistic concepts to teach students about the structure of the English language. I adapted Dr. Postman's work to my own classroom, and was fairly successful at teaching traditional grammar using his linguistic approach. I also wrote several articles describing what I was doing for professional journals.

As a result of those articles, I was invited to present papers at a few professional conferences. I was also invited to teach a demonstration lesson at one of those conferences. Arrangements were made to bring a group of students to the conference, and I taught them in the front of a large conference hall while a group of teachers observed from the rear of the room.

The conference was held on a Saturday, and a friend of mine, a young doctor, came along to watch me "perform." Afterward, over lunch, he asked me, "How often do you do that?" I told him that I taught five lessons practically every day, five days each week.

My friend said, "You're working much too hard. It isn't physically possible to teach that many classes in that way, and to expect to be able to do it for thirty-five or forty years."

I was young, and I was energetic, and I loved teaching. So I continued teaching the way that I had been. And in some ways, I did pay the price, most notably, in my case, by abusing my voice. Certainly, I'm not suggesting that you not work hard. But I am suggesting that you learn to conserve your strength so that you don't "burn out," both physically and emotionally.

COVERING A CLASS

At some point in your career, it will probably be necessary for you to teach a class that is not your own. It may happen occasionally, or it may happen very often. You may be doing substitute teaching early in your career. Or your school may assign teachers to cover the classes of teachers who are absent from school or away on trips.

There are several reasons why covering a class is much more difficult than teaching a class of your own:

- The students in the class know each other, and have developed ways of interacting with one another. You don't know them, and you know nothing about the ways in which they routinely interact with each other.
- You know virtually nothing about the students. You do not know which are likely to participate in classroom activities willingly, and which are likely to "test" you or give you a hard time.
- Unless you are regularly assigned to the school, the students know that they may never see you again.

Your inclination may be to "lay down the law" at the very beginning of the class. While that may work in some situations, I would recommend against it as a general rule. Starting the class by telling students how tough you are may actually make the situation more difficult, particularly if some students see this as a challenge.

So what do you do? The answer is to be well prepared to cover a class long before the situation presents itself. Have several interesting lessons ready, and use whichever seems most appropriate at the time.

I would also recommend that you have some photocopied assignments or projects ready to hand out (word search puzzles geared to the subject and grade level are often ideal). Choose assignments that are neither too difficult nor too easy for the students to complete—you want them to be able to achieve a significant level of success, but you don't want them to finish too quickly. If the students are particularly unreceptive to your lesson, hand out the written assignments. It is amazing how students who otherwise might be inclined to be unruly, will work quietly when they are given a written assignment.

FIELD TRIPS

Field Trips Are a Wonderful Idea

Field trips give students an opportunity to broaden their horizons, to experience something outside of school that they might not otherwise have an opportunity to experience, and to experience it with commentary from their teacher. And a day away from school enables them to return to school the next day renewed and revitalized.

Field Trips Are a Terrible Idea

Field trips are disruptive to the school program, and they are just an opportunity for students, and teachers, to get away from work for a day. And they open the teacher, and the school, to increased liability.

The truth—well, it depends

When field trips are well thought out and implemented, they have all the advantages that are listed in the first paragraph above. But they can be disruptive to the educational program. And no matter how well they are planned, they do open the teacher and school to the risk of increased liability.

If you've decided to take a trip with a group of students, be certain to plan everything well in advance. Trips are one time when you cannot leave anything to chance. Begin by determining the educational objectives of the trip. If the trip doesn't have sound educational objectives, the time will be better spent in school. While a change of scenery might be good for you and for your students, it hardly constitutes a compelling reason for taking a trip.

Once you have determined your educational objectives, your next step should be to plan the trip in detail. I have never seen a school or class trip in which more planning did not result in a better, more trouble-free trip. Begin by answering the following questions:

- Where are you taking the class on the trip?
- Who will accompany you (both adults, and possibly other classes)?
- How will you get there?
- What will you do while you are there?
- How will you return?

Don't skimp here. These questions require more than one-sentence answers. For example, how you are going to get there includes plans for students getting to the departure point, transportation, and getting from the point where students are dropped off, to the site that they will be visiting.

After you have planned out the trip, plan for in-class, pre-trip activities. Certainly, these include instructions for students (and parents) about the mechanics of the trip. But they also include at least one classroom lesson, and preferably an entire unit, which will lead up to the trip and introduce students to the things they will see and experience on the trip.

And, of course, you will want to plan for post-trip activities. Giving students a chance to discuss what they have seen after they have returned to school will make the entire experience much, much more meaningful.

Be certain that you have adequate adult supervision for your trip. This should include a sufficient number of school staff, teachers, teacher aides, and if possible, administrators. And don't neglect to invite a few parents along. Just be sure that parents understand that they need to be available to all students, not only to their own children.

Your school probably has a field trip form that you must submit well before the trip, and also permission forms that must be signed by students' parents. I have seen many otherwise-well-thought-out permission forms that do not ask for an emergency contact telephone number. If your school's permission form does not ask for one, request it yourself. And bring the emergency contact telephone numbers with you on the trip. If the trip will extend beyond regular school hours, be sure that you also have an emergency telephone number for an administrator so that you can contact him if a serious problem develops.

Virtually every permission form contains a statement that absolves the school from responsibility for any injuries or other problems that may occur during the trip. Understand that a school cannot relinquish its responsibility for the welfare of students while they are in its care. And schools are particularly liable in cases in which it is determined that negligence has occurred. Be even more vigilant on a trip than you are in your classroom.

Most field trips come off without a hitch, but still it is a good idea to think about the kinds of problems that can occur, and to plan for them. If you aren't sure, for example, what you would do if a child became sick or was injured on the trip, ask your school administrator for direction before you take the trip.

As a school counselor, I was once assigned to bring a group of high school seniors to the Department of Elections so that they could register to vote. This trip was particularly difficult since I didn't personally know many of the students who were attending. When we returned to the buses for our return trip to school, my worst nightmare occurred—I discovered that two students were missing. We searched everywhere for them, but were unable to find them. Then one student said that he had seen the two meet a friend, and they left with him in his car.

I called the school principal to tell him what had happened before we returned to school. He immediately called the students' parents to alert them to what had happened. Had I not learned what had happened to these two students, I would have called the school principal or administrator in charge and asked for direction. The most appropriate administrative response, I think, would have been to:

- leave one teacher at the site, and have the buses return the other students to the school,
- notify the police that two students were missing,
- notify the parents of the missing students, or
- send an administrator to the site to help the teacher who had remained behind search for the students.

Follow every trip with thank you letters. Students can usually write some of the letters, but be certain to thank people at the site you visited, parents who accompanied you on the trip, and if you used a school bus, the school bus driver. School trips can be a wonderful experience for students and also for their teachers. But they require careful planning and vigilance so that you do not encounter problems that can far outweigh their potential benefits.

WORKING WITH SCHOOL STAFF

It is common knowledge in most business organizations that secretaries and other support personnel play critical roles in the organizations, and are privy to a considerable amount of information that may not be widely known among other employees. Successful executives know that the support staff is critical to their success, and even, to their very survival in the organization. Consequently, successful people at all levels of the organization treat support staff respectfully, and well.

Most school administrators are also well aware of the importance of secretaries, custodians, and other support personnel in the operation of their schools. Some teachers also understand this, but many do not. Or if they do, they act as if it were not the case. Perhaps it's a matter of seeing the professional staff as more important than the support staff. But whatever the reason, if you want to be successful in your work, do not miss an opportunity to let the support staff know that they are important, and that you appreciate them.

When I was a high school counselor, I presented an annual evening program for parents. The program was held in the school cafeteria, and attracted several hundred parents. The custodial staff set up the cafeteria for the program, and when the program ended, they cleaned the cafeteria, and returned it to its original condition. Of course, they were just doing their job. But, there are ways of doing one's job, and then, there are other ways of doing it.

At the end of the program, I always thanked each custodian personally. Then, first thing the next morning I sent the following letter to the chief custodian and the building principal.

The Chief Custodian shared the letter with the four custodial helpers. And the principal told them that a copy of the letter was being added to their personnel files. I sent the letter because I sincerely appreciated the help that I had received from the custodial staff. But I can assure you that the custodial staff was extremely appreciative. And as an added

---

Dear Mr. Wilson,

As you know, last night I presented our annual Financial Aid Night program for students and parents in the school cafeteria. The program was a huge success, with well over five hundred students and parents in attendance.

I would like to commend the entire custodial staff, and specifically Tom Smith, Ed Jones, Edith Walker, and Edna Williams for their outstanding support. They were pleasant and friendly to both me and the people who attended the program. And above all they were extremely helpful and efficient.

Without their dedication and assistance, the program could never have been the tremendous success that it was.

Very truly yours,

(My Signature)

bonus they were always helpful when I needed something done. Extremely helpful!

WHO IS YOUR BOSS?

Working in a school is not always as straight forward as working in some other kinds of organizations. As a teacher, it is not at all uncommon to have many "bosses." When I was a high school counselor I reported to a Department Chairperson, Principal, and District Pupil Personnel Director. And that did not include the Secondary Supervisor, Assistant Superintendent, and Superintendent of Schools. The situation for teachers is generally not very different.

This rarely leads to problems, except in those rare situations in which two of your administrators give you conflicting instructions. Your immediate supervisor, for example, may tell you that there are to be no parties the day before a vacation, while your supervisor in the district office may suggest that you have a party for your students on that very day. What to do?

Of course, each situation is different, but your best option is generally to speak to your immediate supervisor and indicate that the direction you have received from your district supervisor is different from what he has suggested you do. Indicate that you want to do the right thing and need help determining what that is.

In most cases, your immediate supervisor will be sensitive to your situation, and will either tell you to do what the district officer suggested, or will discuss the matter with the district officer. However, if your immediate supervisor "digs in his heels" and tells you that he wants you to ignore what the district officer has said, you have a real problem.

If this happens and there is another local administrator, such as a building principal, explain your plight to him, very tactfully. Again, indicate that you want to do the right thing and need help in determining what that is. If all this fails, you will need to contact the district administrator, and explain your situation. Again, be as tactful as you can—you certainly don't want to end up in the middle of a confrontation between two angry administrators.

CAN YOU BE SUED?

I don't need to tell you that we live in a very litigious society. Someday, someone may allege that you have harmed them in some way and sue you for damages. And whether or not there is any merit to their charges, you will most likely have to obtain legal representation to defend yourself. Obviously, you should be careful about how you conduct yourself, both at work and away from work. But no matter how careful you are, the inevitable may occur at some point in your career.

When I was a school counselor, it was widely suggested that one never close the door to his office when alone with a student. If your door was closed and a student alleged that something improper had occurred in the office, you could have a difficult time defending yourself in a legal proceeding. It was a reasonable suggestion, but that said, I will admit that I occasionally closed the door when I was speaking with a student who was particularly upset. Sometimes you choose to take a chance, and sometimes you don't. Fortunately, I was never subjected to allegations of impropriety or legal action.

While most teachers will never be sued, it is certainly possible that the worst will happen. With this in mind, there are several things that you should know.

- A student or parent who feels that you have harmed them in some way may sue you, the school district, or both you and the school district. In most cases, they will sue the school district simply because the school district has much greater financial resources than you do. But in some cases, they may choose to sue you as well.
- If you are sued in connection with the performance of your job, notify your school administrator, in writing, immediately. In most cases, if you are sued in regard to the performance of your job, your employer must provide you with legal representation.
- You should also notify your teachers' union or teachers' association representative in writing. In many cases they will also provide you with legal assistance.
- Depending on the nature of the charges, you may want to consult with, and possibly retain, independent legal counsel.

- If you are ever sued, do not admit anything, and do not discuss your case with anyone other than your legal representative.

Legal Negligence

Consider the following situation. A group of students are sitting on the bleachers in the school gymnasium, watching a school basketball game. Suddenly, the bleachers collapse. A few students are injured, and sue the school district for the injuries that they have sustained.

Now suppose that the physical education teacher had previously told the school principal that the bleachers were in need of repair, but that the necessary repairs were never made. Should this become known, the school district may be found legally negligent, and the students will very likely be awarded additional damages by virtue of that negligence.

In layman's terms, legal negligence involves either of the following:

- doing something that a reasonable person would not have done in that situation, or
- not doing something that a reasonable person would have done in that situation.

In this example, the court is likely to find the school negligent, because knowing that the bleachers were in need of repairs a reasonable person would have arranged for those repairs to be made in a timely manner.

Protecting Yourself

One way to protect yourself personally is to purchase excess liability insurance (which is often commonly referred to as an umbrella policy) from your insurance provider. Excess liability insurance protects you for a specified amount of money, usually one or two million dollars, for damages in excess of your regular insurance coverage. In other words, it adds to whatever other insurance coverage you have, most notably, your homeowners or renters insurance and your automobile insurance. If you are sued, in most cases it will protect you up to the amount of your policy. Best of all, excess liability insurance is very inexpensive.

DEALING WITH STRESS

I once read an article that related workplace stress to two factors:

- The more people you come into contact with in the course of your work, the more stress you will experience.
- The less control you have in the performance of your work, the more stress you will experience.

The article went on to describe carpentry as a relatively stress-free job. Carpenters don't generally work with many people, and they have a considerable degree of control over how they do their work. Doctors are likely to experience more stress than carpenters because although they have a considerable degree of control over their work, they come into contact with many more people than the average carpenter. Nurses, however, tend to be more stressed even than even doctors because nurses deal with many people in the course of their duties, and because they also tend to have much less control over their work than do doctors.

If this hypothesis is correct, and I think that it is, then teaching is a reasonably stressful occupation. You deal with a large number of students every day, as well as parents, administrators, support staff, and a variety of other people. And you do not have much control over your working conditions.

There are many ways to deal with work-related stress, and I would highly recommend that you experiment with some of them until you find those that work for you. Exercise works for many people, as do sports, yoga, meditation, and music for others. Experiment and you will certainly find some things that work for you.

One exercise that I have found very helpful is a yogic breathing exercise that is promoted by Dr. Andrew Weil in several of his books and on his website (www.drweil.com). You can do it almost anywhere, and it requires no equipment or cost.

Begin by resting the tip of your tongue just above your upper front teeth. Keep your tongue there throughout the exercise.

1. With your mouth closed, count to four slowly as you inhale through your nose.

2. Now hold your breath and count to seven.
3. Finally, exhale through your mouth, making a "whoosh" sound as you count to eight.
4. Repeat the process several times.

Repeat the entire process two or three times each day.

WHAT TO DO IF YOU ARE INJURED AT WORK

As jobs go, teaching is generally considered to be fairly safe. It is certainly much safer than a lot of other kinds of work. But as with any job, it is possible that you will be injured while you are at work. If you are injured, you should know what to do, and what your rights are.

If you are injured on the job, or if you become sick as a result of your work, you should immediately notify your school nurse and/or administrator. They will most likely ask you to complete a Workers' Compensation form—if they do not, ask for one. Complete it carefully, indicating the date and time that you were injured, the nature of your injury, and how it was incurred. Make a copy of the form for your records, and submit the original as quickly as possible.

Each state has its own Workers' Compensation law, so the provisions vary somewhat from one state to another. However, the general concept of Workers' Compensation is that employees who are injured or disabled on the job are provided with fixed monetary awards, eliminating the need for litigation. Workers' Compensation laws also provide benefits for the dependents of workers who are killed in work-related accidents or as a result of work-related illnesses.

If you incur medical expenses, those should be paid under the provisions of the Workers' Compensation law. And if your injury requires you to miss work, you should not be penalized for time that you are away from work.

In many cases, you can handle the process yourself. But if you feel uncomfortable about your ability to do that, or if your injuries are particularly serious, you may want to retain the services of an attorney who specializes in Workers' Compensation cases. In many states, the attorney's fee will be paid as part of your settlement, so you will have no out-of-pocket legal expenses.

Some work-related injuries are fairly obvious. You are lifting a box of textbooks and strain your back, you slip on some debris in the cafeteria, or as a typing or computer science teacher you develop carpal tunnel syndrome. But sometimes your injuries will not be so obvious. Proving that you caught a cold from a sick student would likely be very difficult. But if a student in your class had a particularly contagious illness, and if you developed symptoms a few days after you were exposed to him, you would probably stand a good chance of being compensated.

WHAT TO DO IF YOU ARE ASSAULTED

In some schools, assaults of teachers are virtually non-existent, while in others assaults may occur with considerable frequency. Hopefully, you will never be the victim of an assault. However, it is important that you know what to do in the event that this problem does occur.

First, if you have been injured in any way you must receive medical treatment. If your injuries are even relatively serious, the school will arrange for treatment as they would for anyone who had sustained any injuries on the premises, regardless of the cause. If your injuries are not serious and the school does not arrange for medical treatment, you should seek treatment on your own. It is important that you receive medical treatment even if you have sustained only minor injuries. This will not only ensure that your injuries are not more serious than they appear, but will also provide a record should legal action ensue.

Immediately after you receive medical treatment, prepare a written narrative of the event. Indicate the date and time, the conditions preceding the assault, the nature of the assault, and anything else that may be pertinent. Include the names of potential witnesses, both adults and students.

If you have any injuries, even minor injuries, you should file a report with the school nurse and complete the Workers' Compensation form. Be certain to keep a copy of your completed form for your records. If you require medical treatment, Workers' Compensation benefits will pay for them. And if you miss work as a result of the assault, the time lost should not be deducted from your sick leave.

Meet with the school administrator as soon as possible after the event. Present him with your written narrative, and indicate that you are very concerned about:

- your safety,
- the safety of students in the school, and
- the safety of other staff members.

Ask the principal how the school proposes to deal with the situation. The school may press charges against the student. Some schools will do this as a matter of course, but some will not. If the school does not press charges against the student, you have the legal right to press charges on your own. Some schools will encourage you to do this, but some will just as actively discourage you from doing it. In either case, the final decision is yours to make.

If you do press charges against the student and are concerned about a recurrence, you may also ask the court to issue an order of protection or a restraining order against the student. If you do that and your request is granted, in most cases the school will be required to transfer the student to another school or to exclude the student from school and provide him with education in an alternative setting.

You should also notify your union or teacher's association. In many cases, they will provide you with advice, and possibly legal representation should that become necessary. If you have sustained any significant injury you may also want to discuss the situation with independent counsel.

There have been instances in which a student has assaulted a teacher and then pressed charges against the teacher, alleging that the teacher initiated a physical confrontation. This can happen as a reaction to your having pressed charges against the student, or even if you decide not to institute legal action. In these situations the school will most likely provide you with legal representation since the incident occurred during the performance of your work responsibilities.

Most teachers are never assaulted by students, and with a little luck you will never be the victim of an assault by a student, or by anyone else. Assaults against teachers are relatively rare in most schools. But if the worst does happen, it is critical that you act in a way that protects you both physically and legally.

BODILY FLUIDS

You became a teacher to teach. But you deal with young people—a considerable number of young people—every day. Occasionally there will be an accident and you will be confronted with a student who is bleeding or drooling, has vomited, or has lost control of some bodily function. In the old days it was easy—teachers just did what had to be done. Today, teachers still do what needs to be done. But with the concern about a number of very serious, contagious diseases such as HIV and hepatitis, teachers need to be much more careful.

Your school probably has a policy about dealing with bodily fluids. Ask the school nurse for a copy of the policy, and read it carefully. Long before an incident occurs, you need to know what is expected of you, and what to do in various situations in which you may come into contact with a student's bodily fluids. The bottom line is that on a very practical level you have two responsibilities:

- You must do whatever needs to be done to assist a student who is sick or injured.
- At the same time you need to protect yourself and other students from coming into contact with that student's bodily fluids and the attendant risk of infection.

Some schools issue "bodily fluid kits" and instructions to all school personnel. If your school does, be sure that you have your kit handy at all times. But if your school is one of those schools that does not provide a bodily fluid kit to staff members, ask your school nurse to help you assemble one. The nurse will probably give you the items that you need. But if she does not, assemble one yourself, and be sure that it is always at hand. Fortunately, the components of a bodily fluid kit are readily available and inexpensive.

At the very least, your kit should consist of the following:

- A pair of surgical gloves—the gloves that come with home hair dying kits will not offer suitable protection.
- A surgical type face mask.
- A pair of protective eyeglasses or goggles.
- A few sterile gauze pads—helpful for dealing with scrapes, small cuts, and nosebleeds.
- A plastic bag—for the disposal of soiled or contaminated items.

If a student is injured, send another student for assistance immediately. Have the student indicate that you have a medical emergency. The school nurse, school administrator, and school custodian should all be contacted (the custodian will be needed to clean and disinfect soiled areas).

After the emergency, place all soiled items in a plastic bag, and only then, remove your surgical gloves and place them in the plastic bag as well. Seal the bag and give it to the school nurse. Items contaminated by bodily fluids need to be placed in special "red" containers and disposed of in a rigorously controlled manner. If any items of your clothing have been contaminated, you will need to remove them as soon as possible, and wash them in hot, soapy water.

If the worst happens and you do come into direct contact with a student's bodily fluids, see your doctor or your local or county health authority as quickly as possible. You may need to receive prophylactic treatment for possible infection.

THE ONLY THING THAT REMAINS THE SAME . . .

You have certainly heard it said: The only thing that remains the same . . . is change.

Certainly, in many, many ways teaching is very different from what it was when I was a young teacher. In fact, teaching is very different today from what it was ten years ago. But so is every profession, and every job. A doctor's day-to-day work is very different from what it was ten years ago, so is a lawyer's . . . and so is a grocery store clerk's.

It could be said, I suppose, that change has been a constant throughout history. Imagine how the caveman's (and cavewoman's) life changed with the discovery of fire, how the writer's life changed with the invention of first the typewriter and then the word processor, and how the college student's life changed with the proliferation and availability of information on the Internet.

But in today's world, change is occurring more rapidly than ever before. The personal computer has become a household word in less than a decade. And the Internet and e-mail have become a part of most people's lives in only a few years. Certainly, many changes have improved the quality of our lives. But change has also often made our lives more stressful. Every time we are confronted with a change or an innovation, we need to adapt to it and change the ways in which we do things— usually, ways in which we feel comfortable doing those things.

I am reminded of a teacher who used to visit me fairly regularly when I was a school counselor. Bob had started in the school district when it was still a rural area. In those days, practically everyone in the community knew each other. Students were generally respectful, and the school district was managed in a very casual way. But things had changed dramatically since those days. The school district had grown to many, many times its original size, and Bob was experiencing real difficulty coping. He would tell me, "These students aren't like my students used to be." And he would continue, "And the administrators, they aren't like in the old days."

I told Bob that he needed to try to accept the fact that students and schools are different than they used to be. But Bob just said, "I'm too old to change." Fortunately, Bob had reached retirement age, and he retired a year or two later. I was glad that he was able to retire when he could no longer cope with the changes that were taking place. But I was sad too, because Bob had a lot to offer his students if he could just have been a little more flexible.

Understand that your students next year will be different from your students this year. And your students the year after will be different still. They likely won't be any better, or any worse. They will just be different.

And you will need to be able to adapt, as your students and the world continue to change.

Yes, the only thing that remains the same . . . is change. That is not to say that this is necessarily bad. In fact, it's what keeps teaching exciting. And it's what keeps teachers young.

THE LAST CHAPTER

What we do for ourselves dies with us.
What we do for others and the world remains and is immortal.

THE LAST CHAPTER

Actually, this is not the last chapter. The last chapter is still to be written. It will be written, not at the end of this year, or even at the end of your career, but at the end of the careers and the lives of all the students whose lives you have touched. So this is only the temporary last chapter.

I said in an earlier chapter that teaching is the best job that I have ever had. I hope that the same will be true for you—that it will be the best job that you ever have. Of course, there will be difficult days, and there will be some disappointments along the way. But teaching should enable you to earn a decent living, and it should also enable you to stay young by interacting with young people. And it will enable you to help young people to be better than they were before they knew you . . . and by doing so, to have an impact on eternity.

After all these years, most days I'm still smiling on my way to work and I'm still smiling on my way home. And I'm still learning how to be an even better teacher. Learn from your experiences and from your colleagues. And as you learn new things, share them with your colleagues, and particularly with new teachers. And if you take a moment to e-mail them to me, I'll try to include them in the next edition of this book.

And most of all, I wish you happiness, and I wish you success.

ABOUT THE AUTHOR

Harvey Singer grew up in New York City, where he attended public schools and received his undergraduate degree from the City College of New York. He also has advanced degrees from New York University, St. John's University, and Hofstra University.

This book is based on Mr. Singer's experiences as an English teacher, first in an inner city junior high school, and then in a large city high school. And it is also based on his work as a high school Dean of Students, a school counselor, a school administrator, a college instructor, and a college administrator.